MW00615840

Instead
of
Schooling

Educating for Creativity,
Resilience & Happiness

Caprice Thorsen

Copyright © 2020 Caprice Thorsen

Published by Joyful Action Publishing

All rights reserved. Printed in the United States of America. No part of this book may be reproduced in any manner whatsoever without written permission except in the case of brief quotations embodied in critical articles and reviews.

ISBN: 9781735401515 (paperback)

To Sage and Kayli who inspired me every day with their wisdom, creativity, and resilience.

CONTENTS

Introduction: Expanding Your Horizons: Learning Outside of School

Most adults and parents that I speak with have never considered that there is an option other than school for their kids or themselves. School is viewed as the golden ticket to the good life. This is a cultural myth that keeps us all trapped in an unnatural system of information processing and behavior control. I aim to show you that there are plenty of alternatives to schooling that expand human potential and goodness and can be delivered affordably to all humans.

Most people believe schooling is education. This misunderstanding drives the universal acceptance of forced government schooling. Education and schooling are completely different endeavors.

> *Education*: a natural right to figure out who you are and what your place is in the world so that you can be fully responsible for your own life; pursuit of self-agency.

> *Learning*: an innate capacity to adapt Self to one's environment to grow and thrive. Humans are designed for active learning.

> *Schooling*: society's attempt to control individuals by forcing them to be obedient. Schooling is designed around passive learning.

Schooling, because if fills brains with information, teaches people to believe all of their thinking, essentially blinding them to their ever-present wisdom. True education points people in the direction of their innate wisdom and shows them how to use their analytical thinking to be a tool of wisdom.

It's incredible how much has changed in the past 100 years, and how much hasn't. Technology has expanded our horizons in incredible ways - instant access to information, knowledge, and experts; efficient communication and travel around the globe; automation of more and more tasks. And yet, our school system plods along feeding students information from highly biased, often inaccurate textbooks and requires them to regurgitate the information on tests to prove their intelligence and value to the workplace. Humans aren't designed to learn that way and it's callous to view precious souls merely as future workers.

If you lived in the 1800s, sending your kids to school would be a strange thing. It was something that most families resisted and force was often used to make families send their children to school. Up until the 1930s, most people only attended school through their elementary years.

Many things that were invented in the 1800s continue to be extremely useful: batteries, electric light, bicycles, safety pins, revolvers, machine guns, dynamite, and the zipper among many things. Others are outmoded and have been replaced: the phonograph, typewriter, facsimile machine. The school system which was institutionalized in 1837 remains unchanged.

The bureaucratic school system is the institution that enforces the compulsory education laws of states, provinces, and countries. It was invented and legislated into being in the mid-1800s. It has taken on a life of its own and become a cultural ritual in post-modern life.

We stand at an inflection point in human history where many paradigms and belief systems are being challenged and replaced. Our technological advances often seem to outpace our wisdom in using technology. Insight Learning offers a solution that grows creativity, resilience, empathy, and wisdom - not to mention that it is fun and is the way that we are designed to learn.

If we didn't believe that the path to a good paying job requires schooling and then college, we would be free to pursue our unique path in life. A college degree is the big carrot and stick that keeps K-12 schooling frozen in place. The truth is that you can get into a great college without K-12 schooling and you can be happy and successful without a college degree. There is no standard path to happiness because happiness is an inner state of being.

I wrote this book to share what I have learned over the course of 18 years of home educating my two daughters, getting $500,000 from the U.S. Department of Education to start two K–12 charter schools, co-founding a democratic Sudbury School, starting a self-directed learning center, creating a course on self-directed learning for the California Teachers College, and launching global learning and parent coaching programs for the SelfDesign Learning Foundation.

10 Reasons to Opt Out of School

1. Focus on personal strengths.
2. Preserve the wonder, awe, creativity, imagination, confidence, peace of mind, and joy we are born with.
3. Experience thriving in life, not just surviving school.
4. Learn how to learn.
5. Create something awesome; create the curriculum (not information processing and obeying).
6. Reconnect with your intuition and inner voice.
7. Explore gazillions of free and low-cost learning resources and experiences - that are fun, engaging, and relevant.
8. Remove all limits to your learning.
9. Success in school doesn't equal success in life (avg. GPA of millionaires is 2.9).
10. Learning is easier and more fun than schooling

PART I: Schooling is NOT Education or Learning

Since the beginning, the state of any society is a direct result of its conditioned way of thinking. - Sydney Banks

There are huge efforts that do go into making people, to borrow Adam Smith's phrase, "as stupid and ignorant as it is possible for a human being to be." A lot of the educational system is designed for that, if you think about it, it's designed for obedience and passivity. From childhood, a lot of it is designed to prevent people from being independent and creative. If you're independent-minded in school, you're probably going to get into trouble very early on. That's not the trait that's being preferred or cultivated. - Noam Chomsky

*As our climate heats up, as mountaintops are removed from Orissa to West Virginia, as the oceans fill with plastic and soils become too contaminated to grow food, as the economy crumbles and children go hungry and the 0.001% grows so concentrated, so powerful, so wealthy that democracy becomes impossible, it's time to ask ourselves; **who's educating us? To what end?** - Carol Black*

My Self Education Journey

I am not anti-education. I am highly schooled -- with an MBA in finance from Carnegie Mellon and a BA from the University of Virginia. I just see through the illusion of schooling. I see it for what it is. It is not education; it is social engineering.

My home education journey started when I decided to unschool my first child in 2002, when I was 2 months pregnant. I was an older mom at 35 and was super excited to be having a baby. And then I had this terrible, scary thought. "What am I going to do for this kid's schooling?" I had succeeded at school even though I hated it and was bored silly. College and grad school were better experiences for me, but I felt like I was stumbling around trying to figure out who I was and what I wanted to do with my life.

As I started doing research about alternatives to school, I came upon a speech given by John Taylor Gatto in 1989 when he was named NYC's Teacher of the Year after 30 years of teaching. It blew my mind. Below is an excerpt as published in Sun Magazine.

> *"Schools were designed by Horace Mann and Barnas Sears and W.R. Harper of the University of Chicago and Edward Thorndike of Columbia Teachers College and others to be instruments for the scientific management of a mass population. Schools are intended to produce, through the application of formulas, formulaic human beings whose behavior can be predicted and controlled.*
>
> *To a very great extent, schools succeed in doing this. But our society is disintegrating, and in such a society, the only successful people are self-reliant, confident, and individualistic — because the community life that protects the dependent and the weak is dead."*

The daily misery around us is, I think, in large measure caused by the fact that — as social critic Paul Goodman put it thirty years ago — we force children to grow up absurd. Any reform in schooling has to deal with school's absurdities.

It is absurd and anti-life to be part of a system that compels you to sit in confinement with only people of exactly the same age and social class. The system effectively cuts you off from the immense diversity of life and the synergy of variety. It cuts you off from your own past and future, sealing you in a continuous present, much the same way television does.

It is absurd and anti-life to be part of a system that compels you to listen to a stranger reading poetry when you want to learn to construct buildings, or to sit with a stranger discussing the construction of buildings when you want to read poetry.

It is absurd and anti-life to move from cell to cell at the sound of a gong for every day of your youth, in an institution that allows you no privacy and even follows you into the sanctuary of your home, demanding that you do its "homework."

All of my years of sitting in class watching the secondhand travel move slowly around the clock suddenly made sense. I vowed that my kids would discover who they were and what their gifts and talents were so that they could avoid a mid-life crisis and not waste the first 20 or so years of their lives.

My children have learned outside of conventional school, moving between self-directed homeschooling, alternative learning centers and democratic schools with the exception of one year in public school when my youngest daughter wanted to try it. I have come to realize that my main motivation in keeping my kids out of school went beyond the fact that I hated school and was intensely bored by it: I didn't want my kids to be institutionalized. I have also started many alternative group learning environments because I understand that kids want to be part of a larger community.

In 2004, I co-founded a democratic Sudbury school in North Carolina with three other families. I learned a lot in that experience, mainly that it is difficult for most parents to trust their kids because they have been trained not to trust themselves. Parents got nervous at the freedom that kids are given at a Sudbury school and often missed that it came with a great deal of responsibility.

When I moved to California in 2007, I was determined to create a self-directed learning center that had the benefits of a Sudbury school without what I perceived as its deficits. That was when I read the book *SelfDesign: Nurturing Genius Through Natural Learning* by Brent Cameron. His description of his Wondertree Center in Vancouver, British Columbia inspired me to pick up the phone and request a visit to this alternative learning center. What I loved about SelfDesign is that it focused on the family as the learning unit and replaced the rules that were often quite burdensome in Sudbury (even though they were created by a student-run judiciary committee) with agreements. Several conversations later, I began working with Brent and the SelfDesign Learning Foundation.

In 2011-12, I tried to start two K-12 charter schools in California for SelfDesign. The charter schools were based on SelfDesign's award winning learner-centered educational philosophy and praxis with a focus on social entrepreneurship and community service.

I received $500,000 in highly competitive federal grants from the U.S. Department of Education to start the charter schools. I did my best to get them authorized with an amazing team of experienced educators and administrators by my side and a perfect building. We couldn't get it done. I had to turn away half a million dollars because the local school district and county office of education would not authorize these charter schools. When does an entrepreneur have funding but not permission?

> *"On the one hand, you have SelfDesign which allows children to follow their interests and passion. On the other hand, you have the California Department of Education that requires all children to learn the same things at the same time. I don't think there is a match here... Inherently the idea that you are going to allow students to select their curriculum based on what they are passionate about, it's inherently contradictory to you have to learn these things and you have to learn them in this order." – Roger Rice, Assistant Superintendent, Ventura County Office of Education, February 25, 2012, Ventura County Board of Education public hearing on the appeal for SelfDesign Young Entrepreneurs Soar and LCCC charter schools.*

I found out that the charter school application process in the county where I was living was rigged. We didn't have a chance despite SelfDesign's numerous awards, accolades and track record. I also learned that child-centered, self-directed learning has no place in public schooling.

The superintendent of Ojai Unified School District at the time, Hank Bangser, told me behind closed doors, "I see how SelfDesign teaches kids to love learning, but I don't see how you cover all of the standards."

So, the charter school petitions were not authorized because school board members saw that SelfDesign, which begins with children's interests and passions and then curates learning experiences and curriculum to meet standards was "inherently contradictory" with the California school system which requires all students to learn the exact same thing at the exact same time in a specified, sequential order. And, of course, for every student that attended one of the charter schools, the school district would lose $5,000.

This experience was disheartening and exhausting. I was unable to inject innovation into a school system that looks very much like a factory. So, my daughters continued to learn outside of public school, combining homeschooling with attending self-directed learning centers.

In 2017, I got divorced and moved to South Carolina to be closer to my Dad. My Mom passed away in 2011 and I wanted my daughters to have some time with their grandfather. My youngest daughter, Kayli, chose to go to public school for 7th grade to make friends quickly in this new place. She chose to go to school and I supported her because she is the author of her own life.

She was a "successful" student. The administrators were shocked that she scored in the 97th percentile in English/Language Arts without having had any direct instruction or schooling up to that point. She made some good friends, got on the honor roll, got straight A's (except for a C in art), and joined the cheer team.

She found the schoolwork to be boring and the grind of make-work overwhelming. Our biggest challenge was to keep her from absorbing the fear and shame that were being used as weapons to control the kids and make them comply. My daughter began to fear:

- Being late -- her homeroom teacher would yell "Tardy!" at late students and shame them publicly,
- Going to school without her tablet fully charged -- she would get a tech demerit and too many would result in an office visit with the Principal.
- Having a uniform violation -- they would shame the female students and make them go home.
- Complaining about any assignment -- teachers would say, "life is hard, this is easy in comparison".

- A mean group of boys who bullied her -- the guidance counselor got numerous complaints from many 7th grade girls and said sexual harassment is extremely common in middle school.

What she discovered is that the entire K-8 school was being run by fear and shame. The biggest source of her discomfort was that she could tell that none of the teachers cared about her. They didn't notice how she felt emotionally. The teachers just paid attention to her outputs. My daughter said, "As long as I was producing good numbers, they could care less how I was feeling." When she decided not to return for her 8th grade year, none of her teachers said anything to her.

I began to wonder why public schools are so fear-based. I have come to realize that teachers are trapped in this negative environment where they rely on fear and shame to march kids through a curriculum that is neither interesting nor relevant to the real world.

I began to reflect back on my consulting and leadership coaching career that I started way before I considered having children. In 1999, I started a business strategy consultancy with two colleagues after working for two strategy consulting firms. In 2000, I got certified as a Personal and Professional Coach to add leadership coaching to my work.

Most of the people I coached felt insecure despite their outward success. It seemed like everyone felt like an imposter waiting to be discovered. Insecurity, fear, shame, and anxiety were the norm. I've noticed that insecurity and emptiness is so widespread it is a cultural pathology, not an individual pathology.

Many of the executives who came to me for career guidance told me, "I've played by the rules. I made it to the top and have lots of wealth, yet I feel empty inside. Isn't there more to life than this?" So, I helped successful executives realize that happiness is an inner game. Nothing in the outside world can make you happy.

I started to connect the dots. *We are all trained to be fearful and insecure from a young age.* And I now had an insider view into the culture of public schools through my charter school experience and the eyes of my self-directed daughter.

Schooling controls us with fear and shame for a promised reward in the future. It trains us to ignore our intuition, override our body's signals, and shut down our inner calling as we are taught to misuse our thinking against ourselves. It puts us in small boxes based on labels like "good at math" or "good at English". It doesn't help us discover our innate gift of creativity. I could stop there and say, "Oh, yeah, the broken factory schooling model." However, the psychological effects last into adulthood and seem to haunt us even when we are successful

> *The child in a classroom generally finds herself in a situation where she may not move, speak, laugh, sing, eat, drink, read, write, think her own thoughts, or even use the toilet without explicit permission from an authority figure. Family and community are sidelined, their knowledge now seen as inferior to the school curriculum.*
>
> *– Carol Black*

Schooling Goes Against Human Nature

Humans are Made of Love

Chilean evolutionary biologist, Humberto Maturana called humans homo sapiens-amans amans or "loving man". Maturana tells us that "love is the only emotion that expands intelligence". He says "...we human beings do not like that somebody else should determine what we think or do; we want to learn, reflect, change... when we feel that we want to change based in our own understanding and choice."[1]

Through his research, Maturana discovered that we are biologically wired for reflective autonomy and freedom of choice. Humans are designed to be soul-directed. I purposefully use this term "soul-directed" instead of the more common "self-directed" to be clear that we are not directing our lives from our small fear-based ego but rather the deeper part of our Self that is connected to infinite intelligence.

This is the part of our Self that never changes and has always been observing our life from a neutral, impersonal vantage point. It is our consciousness, our awareness. It is the part of us that is screaming quietly to get up and go play outside rather than sit still at a desk and memorize shapes and colors and labels for things. It is the part of us that begs for a loving teacher to look into our eyes and see who we really are - a soul, not a meat sack carrying a brain that is empty and ready to be filled with information. We are not information processing machines. We are home sapiens-amans amans. Until we are forced to comply with a technological system that is based in fear and control.

There are two forces in life: love and fear. Humans are designed to love. Learning cannot happen in an environment of fear. Why? Because with fear comes our natural fight-flight-freeze response. Our body sends extra blood to our muscles so we can flee or fight, depriving the brain of blood temporarily. Apparently, you need to run fast to escape the saber tooth tiger but don't need to analyze it.

To use fear as an instrument of control is inhumane. So how does schooling do this? (We will answer why it was designed this way in Part 2 of this book.)

The institution of school has stoked our inner fires of insecurity and fear to control us, keep our butts in seats at school doing make-work that we usually don't find interesting or relevant. Threats of bad grades, office referrals, in-school suspension, combined with public ridicule and shame, leave students fearful, stressed, and insecure.

Fear is so powerful that it can be passed down to future generations. Epigenetic inheritance is the process through which characteristics are passed from parent to child. In an experiment with mice, it was found that fearful memories are passed from father to baby. Male mice were made to fear the smell of acetophenone, an artificial chemical, through the use of electric shocks. This fear was passed on to their offspring for at least two generations[2].

If our schools can be viewed as a microcosm for society, we see a strange dynamic at play where individuals are encouraged to compete for the highest grades and GPA so that they can be successful and therefore happy in the future. They are pitted against each other in a strange, artificial, academic contest. It's a confusing soup of collectivism and individual competition with the prize being a fuzzy reward in the future.

Schooling Focuses on Kids' Weaknesses

The root of human suffering is the belief that "I am this small, separate ego and I am not enough". My biggest concern with schooling is that it is emotionally, psychologically, and spiritually abusive. It teaches us that we are not enough. Nobody is good at everything, but schooling forces us to perform in all artificial subject areas according to a made-up timetable. It doesn't matter what our gifts and interests are. We are labeled "good in English" or "good in math" or "good at sports".

We all believe and fear that we are not enough...

- not smart enough
- not beautiful enough
- not skinny enough
- not rich enough
- not loved enough
- not popular enough

You have been trained to compete, fight, cheat, look out for yourself, claw your way to "the top". Research shows that toddlers are naturally cooperative and compassionate (until it is schooled out of them).

We also believe that there is not enough. Not enough to go around:

- not enough money
- not enough love
- not enough friends
- not enough jobs
- not enough appreciation

We take children, put them in a room, separate them from nature and the outdoors, don't allow them to play, bore them with standardized curriculum, force them to sit still, require them to seek permission to go to the bathroom, feed them ideas that are all made up and often incorrect, subjectively grade them, tell them that their personal worth is tied to these grades, and then we ask them to be empathic, compassionate, creative, while excelling in reading, writing, and math.

We never ask children and youth what they are interested in learning, what they enjoy doing, or what their calling or passion is. Most high-school dropouts state their reason for leaving is boredom and knowing that what they are being taught is not relevant to their lives.

In schooling, we break children's connection to their:

- Natural way of learning
- Inner knowing/intuition/common sense
- Cooperative, empathic nature
- Home in nature
- Playfulness
- Love of learning
- Resilience
- Imagination and Creativity
- Awe and wonder
- Soul's calling
- Uniqueness, personal talents and gifts

You have been conditioned to view the world and your Self in a specific way. We have been told that the world is cold and competitive, good jobs are scarce, and you need to look out for #1. This is simply not true unless we think it is and make it so.

We Consume Too Much Because We Are Insecure

We are addicted to fear. The insecurity virus is rampant and contagious. Absorbing fear and insecurity, you try to consume and achieve your way to feeling okay about yourself and earn the permission to love yourself.

Institutions and companies feed on this energy to sell us stuff and "solutions" to cure our insecurity and self-doubt. Companies and their armies of psychologists, advertisers, and marketers feed and stoke our inner fears and insecurities to sell us everything from cars, closets, makeup, cheeseburgers, beer, therapy, and self-help techniques.

We now connect more on the advertising platforms of Facebook, Instagram, and Snapchat more than we do in person.

One of the strongest criticisms of western culture is its over-consumption and resulting environmental degradation of the planet. Schooling created this wacky consumer culture by training us to be consumers whose perceived value increases the more we consume.

> *School is the first impression children get of organized society; like most first impressions, it is the lasting one. Life according to school is dull and stupid, only consumption promises relief: Coke, Big Macs, fashion jeans, that's where real meaning is found, that is the classroom's lesson, however indirectly delivered.*
> *- John Taylor Gatto*

You've been trained by school to see yourself as both the producer and consumer of your own information. Your value in the job market is based on your accumulation of knowledge – that is only demonstrated by proxy with a piece of paper that proves you did your time. 13 years in school gets you a high school diploma. 6 more years might get you a college degree.

Let's see how schooling props up the economy. Our economy and monetary system is based on never-ending growth. Money is created in our fiat system through debt. When someone takes out a loan, money is created. With no debt, there is no money.

For the economy to continue growing, we need people to work for low wages and to spend their wages by continuously buying and consuming stuff. Why do you buy the latest car, smartphone, fashionable clothes, makeup, home decor, and other stuff? Because you believe that it will make you feel better. Why do you strive to climb the corporate ladder? Because you believe that with a higher position, the prestige and more money will make you feel better about yourself.

Our View of Reality is Warped

Knowledge is shaped by social conventions, values, and practices and transmitted to younger generations through schooling and the media.

Mordechai Gordon, author of *Ten Common Myths in American Education*, reminds us of Paolo Freire's insight that knowledge is not a "gift or possession that some individuals have and others lack". He goes on to say, "On the contrary, knowledge is attained when people come together to exchange ideas, articulate their problems from their own perspectives, and construct meanings that make sense to them. It is a process of inquiry and discovery, an active and restless process that human beings use to make sense of themselves, the world, and the relationships between the two."[3]

Humans are meaning makers. We are designed to explore our environment and the world to figure out how we can best grow and thrive. We experience the world through our thinking and assign meaning to our thoughts.

Two of the best ways to explore the world is through free inquiry and conversation. Conversation is the most useful technology that humans have invented for learning. In conversation with self or other, knowledge is expanded. When your mind is at rest, you have an open connection to infinite mind and insights can pop into your consciousness. This is not how modern schooling is designed. Kids are not allowed to speak in school nor are they permitted to freely explore areas of interest or passion.

Schooling Gives A Highly Biased Picture of Reality

Parents expect that the knowledge that is being transmitted to their children in school is true, factual, and unbiased. Unfortunately, it is none of these things. The bias in education is based on the belief systems of materialism, humanism, and socialism.

One problem with schooling using primarily textbooks and tests to teach is that it presents a view of reality as if it is the truth. Knowledge is never value-free. All ideas are made-up. What was once regarded as common knowledge by a previous generation is now viewed as inaccurate or completely wrong. We must admit that what previous civilizations and generations believed have been debunked.

Mordechai Gordon sums it all up nicely: "Since in almost all cases it is the dominant class that controls the media, advertising companies, book publishers, and other information producers, it is, in effect, able to determine what is considered knowledge. An obvious example is the mainstream media in the United States which is controlled by a handful of corporations and very wealthy individuals. Since the vast majority of news in this country is being produced by a few media giants, it is they who ultimately control people's knowledge of both domestic and international affairs. And since the livelihood of the media corporations is dependent on the advertising contracts they obtain, they rarely report news that would offend their advertisers.[4]"

I learned recently that USA Today is owned by Japanese megacorporation Softbank. Here is what you need to understand: you cannot trust the information that is being reproduced by schooling and the media. It is a very skewed version of reality.

The largest teacher's union in the country, the National Education Association is highly political. To confirm this, read the NEA's 2018-19 Principles on the website, which take a highly politicized stance on everything from immigration, abortion, health care, and overthrowing the white supremacy culture. Here's an excerpt:

> *"The National Education Association believes that, in order to achieve racial and social justice, educators must acknowledge the existence of White supremacy culture as a primary root cause of institutional racism, structural racism, and White privilege.[5]"*

Depending on where you fall in the political spectrum, you may think this is incredibly important work or misguided. It is not my intention to have this debate here, but rather to awaken you to the fact that the NEA has a political agenda and is the union for 3.2 million public school teachers in the United States.

Schooled People Maintain the Status Quo

Students in K–12 schooling and college make few cognitive gains, aren't learning useful life skills, and aren't enjoying the process, so why do we force them to spend the first 24 years of their lives in school?

Schooling produces the people who maintain the status quo and prop up our growth-driven consumer economy. Schooled people will work at mundane jobs for low wages and consume all the stuff that our economy needs to sell to survive. It was designed this way.

Am I the only one who sees the extreme foolishness of this business of breaking children's spirits with the belief that there is a body of knowledge they need to memorize? The harm of using arbitrary, subjective grades to determine the value of a person? To put them in a collectivistic environment that forces them to compete as individuals all doing the same thing that none of them chose to do.

It's all completely absurd. People are suffering because their souls have been schooled and their minds have been institutionalized.

The Purpose of Education

*"The goal of real education is to bring us to
a place where we take full responsibility for our
own lives." - John Taylor Gatto*

This is a worthy debate to have. Why do we educate our young? Birds show their young to fly, wild cats show their young to hunt, humans show their young how to live by including them in adult society. Young people discover who they are and how they can function successfully in the world by participating in it. We don't teach humans how to learn. The mind is not a muscle that needs to be exercised. And it is not a machine that needs to be filled with information. In fact, filling it with information can block our ability to receive wisdom.

We come into this world as free beings connected to our innate wisdom and wellbeing. We let our thoughts and emotions pass through without hooking us. We have free will and choose where to focus our attention. We are free from fear and do not judge. We are naturally curious, resilient, altruistic, cooperative. We thrive in nature and through play. Energy flows through our body, encouraging us to move.

Humans are designed to learn so that they grow into self-sufficient beings who self-direct their learning and lives. Learning is a natural, internal process of awakening to Self that best happens as the free inquiry of a relaxed, peaceful, playful mind. We need to trust that humans are designed to learn, and desire is the calling of their soul to learn something. It may be dance, painting, building, writing, or molecular biology. The point is that it is their choosing.

Learning to talk is the most difficult cognitive process and humans master this without anyone teaching them. You are designed to cooperate with your environment and continuously gather knowledge to learn how to best adapt to your current circumstances. Learning is not an object or thing that can be tracked and measured. It cannot be forced.

Indigenous people understood this, so children learned in the community, observing adults, modeling their behavior, and adapting to their environment. Children in industrialized countries are forced to adapt to the artificial, pathological environment of schooling away from the rest of society. *As they grow, they awaken to an artificial self.* They are taught to survive school and not thrive in life.

Many people believe that formal education within a school institution where a teacher is leading the educational activity is the only worthwhile endeavor. Most parents have been conditioned to think that they are incapable of educating their children.

Often, I encounter mothers who look at me and say how brave I am for home educating my kids. Or they ask me how I can stand being with my kids every day. What this points to is a widespread misunderstanding of learning and education.

True education produces secure, independent, literate people who can think for themselves and have self-agency. Education done well is mastery of Self, evolution of consciousness, exploration of gifts and talents, and complete well-being (mental, emotional, physical, psychological, spiritual, and financial). Notice that this list doesn't include information processing and mastery of subject matter.

Education can guide you to understand how your mind works, what your innate skills and talents are and how you want to contribute your gifts to society. Education is not a group activity; it is an individual process that can be greatly enhanced by belonging to an educational community.

People survive in this complex society by using their minds and reason so that they can get their needs met. After the age of 18, it is up to the individual to take action to get needs met. Because we are a species that lives in complex social groups, unless you are living on a self-sufficient farm off the grid, you need to learn to live in society among your fellow humans.

Your ability to successfully navigate this complex society and pursue happiness depends upon your ability to use your mind, connect with your inner wisdom, think critically, and practice self-care. By educating yourself, you get to know yourself and the world, learn how to think, and gradually become responsible for your own life.

The Right to Educate Yourself

The right to educate yourself is a natural human right, not one given to you by any government. Notice I didn't say the right to schooling is a natural human right. Schooling is an institution that was invented by men. Education is required by nature for each individual to learn how to adapt to their unique environment.

Every child writes the story of their life and needs to be able to ask essential questions about it. Education encourages you to explore the philosophical questions: Where did life come from? What is my purpose? Is there a God?

One reason that schooling is destructive is because it pretends to have the answers to these questions. Schooling is designed around false existential certainty and pretends that there is a set body of knowledge that needs to be memorized. Absent from school is the acknowledgement that there are as many theories of the origin of life and consciousness as there are scientists. Scientists know nothing about 96% of matter in the universe -- dark matter. And most of the scientific theories become obsolete as human consciousness evolves.

The founding of the United States was a revolutionary experiment to protect people from the excesses of governments and monarchies. The U.S. Constitution was written to protect people from the government and its abuses. Nearly 250 years after the Constitution was written, one-third of Americans cannot name any of the rights in the Bill of Rights and 43% don't know that freedom of speech is a right.[6]

Education reformers will say that this means that school is failing, and we need more money and smaller classrooms. School is succeeding. The results we have gotten from school for the past 100 years are the results it was designed for. Schooling was designed to create a totalitarian socialist society. It goes against the principles and beliefs that the United States was founded on.

We hold these truths to be self-evident, that all men are created equal, that they are endowed by their Creator with certain unalienable Rights, that among these are Life, Liberty, and the pursuit of Happiness.
– The Declaration of Independence

Today, if you are not legally homeschooling your children or have them in a public or private school, the government will take your children from you. So, do you really think that you are free?

Forced government schooling cannot exist in a just society. People with a socialist belief system will claim that schooling levels the socio-economic playing field. It certainly does not. Research shows that schooling perpetuates economic inequalities.

With the explosion of learning opportunities and information available on the Internet, learning can happen anywhere and anytime. Online courses and schools, free open courses from prestigious universities, games-based learning, Maker Clubs, 3D printing, and coding schools are low-cost options that can be made available to everyone for a lot less than the $13,000 we spend per student per year for schooling.

Begin by De-Schooling Yourself

I had to ignore my inner knowing to survive school. Regaining a connection to my soul and inner purpose has been an interesting journey.

Fortunately, humans are designed to thrive. This book isn't just about the mechanics of successful education outside of schooling, it is about the joy of learning and living. Our design is beautiful and magnificent. Not even schooling can break our spirits.

If you were schooled into thinking that your self-worth is attached to performance, achievement, grades, teacher approval, then it's time to wake up and re-jigger your estimation of yourself. There is no correlation between success in school and success in life. The average GPA of millionaires is 2.9.

If you continue to believe that your self-worth is connected to your stuff (house, car, job title, clothes, etc.), your credit score, your performance review, or your number of social media friends, then it's time to wake up and start living your own life.

If you were schooled to think that you are a passive participant in your own life, it is time for you to begin to create the life that you want to live. And stop schooling your kids. The "I suffered through it, they will too" argument is just a symptom of the Prisoner's Dilemma.

> *All I am saying in this book can be summed up in two words—Trust Children. Nothing could be more simple - or more difficult. Difficult, because to trust children we must trust ourselves - and most of us were taught as children that we could not be trusted.*
> *- John Holt, How Children Learn*

The False Beliefs You Were Taught by Schooling

Myth #1: You are alone in a cold, uncaring world.

The schooling paradigm is built on a story of separation. As Charles Eisenstein so clearly tells us, we need to move to a story of Interbeing. As long as we believe that we are separate blocks of physical matter that need to compete for scarce resources (grades, honor roll, GPA, jobs, money, status, stuff) then we will continue our fear-based journey of trying to control all of our experiences so that we feel okay and safe.

It's not your fault. You have been conditioned to view the world in this way and are doing the best you can inside of this false worldview.

We are stressed, anxious, fearful, depressed, apathetic, and lonely.

Myth #2: Human thinking is not a creative force.

We are conditioned to use reactive thinking, not creative thinking. Things happen and we react, then we think and say, "Well of course I'm upset, you would be upset too if you had the same experience." Life becomes a continuous reaction to outside stimuli. You are sad or happy and decide if life has meaning or is meaningless using what happens to you day to day as evidence.

Experiences do not cause thoughts. Experiences give you the perfect opportunity to be upset, sad, angry, happy, or peaceful. Experiences do happen. Once over, they are gone and live only in your thoughts. But we innocently believe that experiences mean something.

We are the creators of meaning. Human thought is the most powerful force in the world. It creates our life stories through our beliefs and habitual thoughts. When we change our relationship to our thinking, we are free to write an awesome life story and enjoy every moment. Most of us are unaware that we are the thinker, we believe all of thinking because it produces strong emotions and sensations that feel true. You are not your thoughts.

We live in our heads, constantly processing information, hoping for peace and happiness at the end of a thought storm. We are deprived of the joy of being alive.

Myth #3: Your intellect defines who you are

Our brains are fabulous tools of our greater mind that we can use to process and analyze information. Schooling, with its endless information processing and analyzing, blinds us to our greater mind and the wisdom that is always available to us. We are trained like flesh-covered robots to process information and obey. Your self-worth is measured by how much information you process. Humans are not designed for information processing.

The artificial measuring stick of schooling makes us all feel like impostors.

Myth #4: Life is to be conquered, not to be held sacred

When kids are allowed free time in nature, they stay enchanted with the natural world. If they are able to engage in fresh scientific discovery and philosophical debates, they will love learning. Schooling pretends that adults have figured it all out and a kid's job is to memorize the facts of life. Did you know we are in the middle of a new scientific revolution that will turn everything you think on its head? This makes standards, standardized curriculum, and testing an incredible waste of time and resources.

A boring, rigid schooling system blocks free play, nature immersion, inquiry, philosophy, and conversation. We lose the awe and wonder of being alive and creative.

Myth #5: You need to obey

You've been psychologically manipulated to obey no matter what cost. School's laser focus on standardized information processing requires a culture of coercion. Teachers are forced to march kids through standardized, mind-numbing, often inaccurate curriculum. Schooling takes away our free will and the power of choice. We are not allowed to choose what we think, what we learn, how we learn it, who our teachers and mentors are.

We're busy chasing a false promise of future happiness and obeying outside authorities while our lives slip by.

What Do You Believe?

If you believe that...

There is no creative force, higher power or God in the universe.

Science and technology are the supreme powers that will solve all earthly problems.

Children enter the world as completely blank slates, with no soul or calling.

They will become bad and useless unless trained otherwise.

Children must be forced to learn because they are lazy.

We need to be controlled by a powerful, centralized state that is led by self-chosen elites, otherwise it will be chaos.

An under-educated class of workers–consumers is an essential part of the design.

Then forced government schooling is your solution.

If you believe (like me) that...

Life is a wonderful, awe-inspiring mystery and chances are good that there is a universal intelligence, consciousness, or God that exists.

Humans are part of nature, not outside of it or above it.

The use of technology is best moderated by wisdom.

Humans are naturally curious and designed to learn.

Children are inherently resilient, cooperative, and empathic.

Each child is unique with gifts, talents, a calling and a purpose.

Human creativity, ingenuity, and entrepreneurship are positive forces that can be encouraged and expanded.

People have an innate drive to create, not consume.

Then begin your true education journey and choose the flavor that best fits your family: unschooling, homeschooling, an alternative learning center, or a hybrid approach.

Explore Your Why

What is your why? It's okay if you aren't clear at this moment. As with anything in life, once you get really clear about your why, it becomes easier to stay the course when you hit bumps in the road. And you will have glorious days and ones where you wish you would have stayed in bed.

I believe that the goal of education is empowered, awakened individuals who use their minds, creativity, and energy to co-create a free and fair society and healthy biosphere. I see that schooling is more geared towards molding compliant citizens who will be effective workers. I invite you to create a why for your family that is separate from the agenda of schooling.

I read an excellent book by Jon and Myra Kabat-Zinn soon after my first daughter was born called *everyday blessings: the inner work of mindful parenting*. I highly recommend it! For me, it reframed my mothering journey as a spiritual one. This helped on the day that my youngest daughter, not yet 2 at the time, bit me three times. Ouch!

My why for home educating my daughters has changed over the years. First, it was to protect them from the sheer boredom of schooling and give them time and space to discover themselves. Later, I realized that I wanted them to be able to think for themselves and didn't want them to be institutionalized.

I led a workshop at the California Homeschool Association conference in 2009 entitled *Trust*. It was focused on helping parents learn to trust their kids and the natural learning process. I started the workshop by asking parents what they truly wanted for their kids. The consensus was they all wanted their kids to be happy. Nobody mentioned good at math, writing, or social studies. So, I'm guessing that you are home educating or considering home educating your kids because you love them and want them to be happy. That's enough of a why for anyone.

What are Your Own Schooling Wounds?

To joyfully home educate your children, you need to recognize that you got some wounds in your schooling experience. Kirsten Olson wrote an excellent book called *Wounded By School*. She set out to interview successful people and find out how their school experience contributed to their success. She discovered that everyone had deep wounds from school and succeeded in spite of their schooling. Peter Gray offers an excellent summary in his Psychology Today Blog

I co-created a global coaching program for homeschooling families and quickly learned that we all believe our school experience was somehow lacking. We then try to make up for what we didn't get by giving whatever we were missing to our children. It's helpful to see if we are trying to meet our old, unmet needs or the current needs of our individual children. You will learn this through trial and error. Give yourself permission to be flexible so that you can change course quickly when something is not working. As we will explore in Ages and Stages, your child's needs will change over time.

I had no freedom in school, so I gave my daughters lots of freedom. My oldest daughter enjoys structure and someone to choose her projects for her, so I learned to create enough structure and guidance for her so that she feels safe. My youngest daughter is highly self-directed and wants ultimate freedom. So, even in your home, you will adjust the environment to meet individual needs.

One mom that I coached had attended a free school in the desert of New Mexico. She felt that her school experience was too loose and that she didn't get the academic rigor that she wanted, so she initially chose a highly regimented, academically focused program for her kids. She didn't realize that she was trying to meet her own needs not those of her children.

By recognizing your own wounds and unmet needs, you can own them for yourself and not project them onto your kids. My wounds in school are all of the psychological variety. See if any of these are familiar to you.

I often feel insecure. After years of competing for grades and high GPAs, I have been trained to compare myself to other people. I know that this is a losing game, but it seems to have been drilled into me. There will always be someone that looks more successful or better than me, so I have to remind myself that I am using my thinking against myself. I feel insecure because I am having insecure thinking and this was encouraged in school.

I'm afraid to be late. The tyranny of the bells in school and fear of missing the school bus still activate fear in my body.

I hate making a mistake. I believe that it shows I am somehow worthless. I see how school only rewards the right answer and an A is much better than a C, even if you only learned something long enough to do well on a test. I'm just giving myself permission to make mistakes because I know that is the only way to learn something new.

I fear the unknown. I often procrastinate when starting something new because I don't already know how to do it. I see how schooling discouraged risk taking.

Schooling is an unnatural way of learning that forces kids to learn the same things and the same time irrespective of interest or ability. Because schooling is so excruciatingly boring and irrelevant, teachers resort to fear and shame to coerce kids to jump through antiquated academic hoops.

We have been conditioned to value ourselves by arbitrary grades created by outside authorities. If we got bad grades, we think we're stupid. If we got good grades, we will often stay on the performance and achievement treadmill for life. It doesn't matter that only 5% of people learn in the auditory-sequential-symbolic way that school teaches information. Most of us secretly harbor the belief and fear that we are not okay. We were taught this in school.

Our culture is increasingly fear-based. Negative thought patterns about self and the world are reproduced and reinforced in school.

Overcoming Your Fear of Making a Mistake

When deciding about their children's education, most parents make a decision based in fear. They are afraid of making a mistake and their children will be left behind. Fear is always an indication that you are thinking fearful thoughts, but it has nothing to do with the outside world unless you are encountering a bear or a snake.

Learn to trust the natural learning process. Your child has innate wisdom that is always guiding her just like you have innate wisdom guiding you. I talk about self-directed education frequently, and here I am going to switch gears and call it soul-directed learning.

I lost count of the time another mother has told me how brave I am to homeschool my children. And yet, as August approaches, they tell me that they are hoping their child gets a good teacher and laments the bad teachers from last year or the kids that bullied their child. To me, they are playing Russian Roulette with their child's education. I have never had to hope that my kids will get a good teacher or not get bullied.

And I don't put pressure on myself to be a perfect teacher, because I am more of a guide on the side. I encourage their interests, I strew books and materials around the house, and most importantly, I operate from love not fear.

As I will show in the following chapters, there are no "basics" to master, there is no critical information to memorize, there is no way that your child will fall behind. Learning is not a race. There are no winners. There are young people who are enchanted with the world, love to play, and are naturally wired to learn and grow.

Brent Cameron, co-founder of SelfDesign, often likened schooling to gluing wings to a caterpillar. It just doesn't work. In his famous TED talk, Sir Ken Robinson shows how schools kill creativity and points out that our school system is designed to produce college professors.

Debunking the School-Job-Happiness Myth

We submit to schooling because there is a strong bias against people who don't have a college degree and we have been fed the myth that this is the path to happiness.

The School-Job-Happiness Myth is deeply flawed and destructive to many generations. Even if education does lead you to a high-paying job, who says that you will be happy?

In my work as an executive coach, many of my clients have been adults in their 30s, 40s, and 50s who were well paid in the corporate world and struggling to find meaning, purpose and joy in their lives. I also don't think that most people want to work only 4 hours a week and lounge on the beach. This might be cool for a few months, but then our natural desire to be connected to a higher purpose kicks in.

High school is failing many young people. In the 2015 Gallup Student Poll of students in grades 5-12:

- 50% are not engaged or actively disengaged in school.
- 52% feel stuck or discouraged.
- Only 25% of high school students are learning how to start a business.

The 2016 Gallup Student Poll shows that 34% of 12th graders are engaged, 35% are not engaged, and 32% are actively disengaged in school.[7] We can easily connect the dots between this and the fact that, in 2018, only 34% of adults were engaged in the workplace.[8]

And there is a parallel in corporate American today. Gallup's State of the American Workplace survey finds that only 13% of adults are "engaged" at work - they look forward to it and believe it is meaningful. The rest are sleepwalking through their workday, waiting for the weekend (63%) or they hate it (24%).

Johann Hari, author of *Lost Connections: Uncovering the Real Causes of Depression – and the Unexpected Solutions*, found that people who don't believe their work is meaningful and feel they have no control over their time and activities in their workplace are more likely to be depressed and stressed. He recommends focusing on the power imbalances in the workplace rather than a theoretical chemical brain imbalance in individuals.

The Taboo Against the Self-Educated

I was extremely bored and found most of what I learned in school to be irrelevant. And I am not alone. Elon Musk hated school and called it torture. So, he started a new type of school for his sons at SpaceX. He's not sending them to public or private school.

Unfortunately, there is a taboo against the self-educated. School is a new social construct that has become the norm over the past 100 years. Self-education used to be the norm. George Washington, Abraham Lincoln, and Thomas Edison were all self-educated.

Bryan Caplan, an economist and author of The Case Against Education says that a college degree is mainly a signaling device of employability because you don't get any social creds for doing one or two years. He makes a good case.

"Education is a waste of time and money because so much of the payoff for education isn't really coming from learning useful job skills. Nor is it coming from students savoring the educational experience. Rather, most of what's going on is that people are showing off — or, as economists call it, they are "signaling." They are trying to impress future employers by showing how dedicated they are." – Bryan Caplan,

If children aren't gaining useful skills and aren't enjoying the process, then why do we force them to spend the first 24 years of your life in school? These are the years when humans have the most energy, creativity, and imagination. Until it is schooled out of them.

If college admissions looked different, then K-12 schooling would most likely have different standards. High schools across the country added Algebra and Geometry as a graduation requirement after Harvard made these courses an entry requirement. The powerful University of California system has a list of required A-G high school classes that one must pass to attend a UC school. K-12 schooling is currently designed to transmit inert knowledge so that students get good scores on tests and the SAT/ACT.

In the U.S., the only socially acceptable path into adulthood is still college. And the better the college, the brighter the prospects. Many parents live in fear that their children won't get into a "top" university and therefore never have a good chance at success and riches. From this fear, they reverse engineer all their education decisions. They focus on grades and often over-schedule their children with extracurricular activities to make sure that their kids can get into a prestigious college.

Let's take a moment to examine this. I'm not opposed to higher education. I got a BA at University of Virginia and an MBA in finance from Carnegie Mellon University. College is best approached as part of a larger plan. It is an expensive proposition to hope that a person will discover her gifts and talents at university. A few do. Most don't.

College Doesn't Offer Everyone a Positive ROI

70% of students from half of the colleges in the U.S. make less than high school graduates[9]. Let that sink in. Read the source data.

The belief that getting into a good college will guarantee you a job and financial security is misguided. 25% of recent college graduates are unemployed and have an average of $27,000 in college loan debt.

Student loan debt will only be forgiven if they work for 5 years for the government, a non-profit, or an education institution. What a scam! Really? Why would a bankruptcy court forgive the credit card debt that you used to buy a flat-screen TV but not the Fannie Mae loan you got to pay for your college education? College and university tuition rates have skyrocketed in correlation to the ease of getting student loans.

In my initial research on ROI, I have found that 40% of liberal arts majors are working in jobs that don't require a degree. It's not necessarily true that STEM careers are the way to go. On average, those who pursue TEM (technology, engineering, maths) education and careers have a positive ROI on their college tuition. S degrees (biology, zoology, geology, etc.) do worse than some social science and English majors. Social science majors often fare well in the long-term because they get advanced degrees. However, I have many friends with mounds of debt from this strategy.

By now you might be thinking, "OK – Caprice, it's fine if you want to risk your daughters' futures by telling them that they don't need to go to college. But, I'm certainly not that stupid." Here is what I say to my daughters, "If on your chosen path, it makes sense for you to go to college, I will support you and help make it happen."

When my oldest daughter is at dance class, I sometimes park myself and my laptop at Barnes & Noble to do some work. Almost every table at the connected Starbucks has a high school student getting math tutoring. Irrespective of your thoughts on kids struggling, sweating and crying over their math homework, it's good to know that many famous scientists and inventors struggled with maths the way it is taught in school.

Einstein and Edison are two famous examples of people who succeeded wildly in life and failed at school. Edison was called "addled" by his school master, Mr. Crawford, and Edison begged not to have to go back to school. He then was taught at home by his mother, but hated maths instruction so avoided it.

> *"I can always hire a mathematician, [but] they can't hire me." - Thomas Edison*

"School failed me, and I failed the school. It bored me. The teachers behaved like Feldwebel (sergeants). I wanted to learn what I wanted to know, but they wanted me to learn for the exam." – Einstein and the Poet

The main reason that kids drop out of high school isn't because they are failing. It is because they are bored and find what they are learning to be irrelevant.

The trouble is most of the stuff that kids learn in college doesn't prepare them for a successful life or career. And usually, college graduates focus on getting good paying jobs to pay off their new student loans. So, most college graduates cannot even follow their callings, if they were lucky enough to discover them while spending 7+ hours a day at school.

I had a double major in cultural anthropology and international relations at University of Virginia then got an MBA in finance at Carnegie Mellon. I was told that liberal arts was the way to go because it teaches you to think. College isn't about getting a job or contributing to the economy. It's about expanding your intellectual capacity and expanding your horizons. Well, maybe that was true in the 1980s and 1990s before the widespread availability of online MOOCs, YouTube, and coding schools. Today you can learn anything online.

However, in 2020, I can certainly think of thousands of more affordable ways to increase your intellectual capacity, broaden your horizons, and build concrete skills than going to college. And they can all be self-directed by each individual according to her learning style, interests, and optimal pace of learning.

K-12 schools point to college as if it is a requirement for a successful career or a fulfilling life. Parents are fed fear-based myths about what will happen to their children if they don't go to college. Much of this is funded by sophisticated marketing and PR campaigns.

Let's Evolve Human Consciousness

We have a fundamental responsibility to awaken and educate young people in a way that evolves human consciousness. To change the trajectory of the human project, we need a new narrative of who we are, how learning happens, and what it takes to create a just and free society. To do this, we have to challenge the current paradigm that leads to separation, fear, and the quest to control life.

When we educate to preserve innate wholeness, wisdom and wellbeing, young people will unleash their unlimited capacity to innovate. They can evolve the world and society in a positive direction through their insights.

Humans are born:	Until they are conditioned to become:
INNOCENT	UNETHICAL
WISE	UNAWARE
CURIOUS	APATHETIC
SECURE	INSECURE
CREATIVE	CONSUMERS
COOPERATIVE	COMPETITIVE
ALTRUISTIC	SELFISH

The fatal flaw of the schooling paradigm is that it was designed from FEAR. When you look at direct quotes from the men who invented and championed government schooling in the mid-1800s and early 1900s, their fear and arrogance is visible. Children are treated like deficient machines that need to be molded into productive citizens that can be controlled. In this game, the student who is the most obedient and processes the most information wins.

Children are being conditioned to survive school rather than thrive in life. Schooling falsely claims that learning is a mechanical process best undertaken in neo-Darwinistic competitive individualism same-age classrooms following standardized curriculum.

PART 2: Schooling is a Losing Game

The dirty underside of our system is that schools as we know them today are structurally designed to fail a reliable percentage of kids. Interestingly, they reliably fail a much higher percentage of kids in low-income areas than they do in affluent areas, and this is true from Detroit to Gilgit-Baltistan. - Carol Black

If the world has not come to its end, it has approached a major turn in history, equal in importance to the turn from the Middle Ages to the Renaissance. It will exact from us a spiritual upsurge, we shall have to rise to a new height of vision, to a new level of life where our physical nature will not be cursed as in the Middle Ages, but, even more importantly, our spiritual being will not be trampled upon as in the Modern era. This ascension will be similar to climbing onto the next anthropologic stage. No one on earth has any other way left but -- upward. - Aleksandr Solzhenitsyn

Schooling vs. Living: Two Contradictory Paradigms

This chart shows you the way in which schooling contradicts how life really works. If this is confusing at first, don't worry. It will make sense soon. Once you see it, you cannot un-see it.

	Belief System of Schooling	How Life Really Works
Narrative of the World	Separation	Unity
How Life is Organized	Into separate blocks of inert matter. You are alone in a cold, uncaring world	All of life is intelligent energy that cannot be separated. You are like a wave on the ocean of life.
Orientation of Experience	Outside In	Inside Out
Consciousness	Local. Located inside the brain. Inert matter creates consciousness. Ends with death.	Non-local. Consciousness creates matter. Continues after death.
Power of Thought	Thinking is passive and describes a fixed outside reality.	Thinking creates your individual reality. Change your thinking and change your life.
Emotional Intelligence	Circumstances evoke emotional	Emotions and sensations indicate

	responses and body sensations within us. Learn to manage your emotions and reactions.	your level of thinking. They don't have anything to do with your circumstances.
Being Present	Future orientation. Do school today for rewards in the future.	The Power of NOW. The only thing that exists is the present moment. Stay fully open to the beauty of the now.
How Learning Happens (or not)	Information Processing, Give the Right Answer, Testing	Doing, Trial and Error, Play, Conversation
Self-Worth	Earned through Performance	Innate
Existential Questions	Adults have figured it all out. Just memorize the answers. Become disenchanted with the world.	Explore, Converse, Decide. Embrace the mystery of life and remain in awe and wonder.

How to Navigate Life	Let your intellect guide you. Use your brain to analyze every situation. Live in your head.	Let your innate wisdom guide you. Your brain is a receiver that is connected to universal intelligence.
The Good Life	Acquisition & Consumption	Creation & Connection

As you look through this chart, can you see that the way life and nature really work is the opposite of how schooling was designed in the 1800s and early 1900s?

Schooling: A Fearful Experiment that Became a Cultural Norm

How did this collectivist, fear-based model of education come to be and why don't we view children as precious souls with unique callings in life? Why aren't we educating them to be self-reliant and self-directed?

What I discovered as I explored this question was that schools were institutionalized by men in the mid-1800s who put themselves above the rest of humanity in order to arrange and regulate people. They believed that humans were inert raw material that could be molded into something. They chose to play God and be the molders of other people.

It is one thing for a man or group of men to decide that a school of their invention would benefit some children. They have a right to their ideas. And they have a right to employ their own resources to create these schools and invite families to pay for these schools.

But that's not what they did. They used the power of law to force all children to attend the schools that they invented, borrowing inhumane practices from India and the Soviet Union and used taxpayer money to fund their artificial institutions.

The totalitarian communist Leon Trotsky (a Soviet communist revolutionary) revered the father of American schools, John Dewey. The way that schools were described in the Soviet Union in the early 1900s is almost identical to how they are described in the United States today.

Anyone who loves liberty and believes in justice and freedom needs to look at schooling from a different perspective. Rather than educating and empowering people, schooling breaks human spirits and creates fearful, dependent people who cannot separate fact from fiction.

The men who invented and championed forced government schooling in the 19th and 20th Centuries knew exactly what they were doing. They believed that human nature was corrupt, that life is random - not a gift from a higher power, and that they could create a Utopian society by controlling people. Their dogmatic beliefs in scientific materialism and reductionism, religious humanism, and socialism made it perfectly okay to force children to submit to schooling.

Most humans are empathic beings. The exception being those who have a personality disorder (narcissistic, anti-social, and borderline) or psychopathy. When the men in the 1800s set out to create a utopian society, they didn't understand human nature.

> *Empathy is the opposite of utopia… There is no empathy in utopia because there is no suffering. Empathy is grounded in the acknowledgement of death and the celebration of life and rooting for each other to flourish and be. It is based on our frailties and our imperfections. So when we talk about building an empathic civilization we are not talking about utopia. We are talking about the ability of human beings to show solidarity not only with each other but our fellow creatures who have a one and only life on this planet. We are homo empathic.* – Jeremy Rifkin

Generations continue to be robbed of their imaginations, curiosity, love of learning, natural genius, and the ability to author their own lives by a school system that was not designed for learning. It was designed for compliance. I don't hear lots of CEOs asking for obedient, compliant workers who blindly follow orders.

Schooling damages people and limits their views of themselves. School creates within people a deep sense of insecurity and fear. Endless comparisons, competition, grades and testing are inhumane and teach people that their self-worth can be shown on a bell curve. The school system has nothing to do with real, lasting learning.

Fear: The Roots of Schooling

There are two creative forces in the world: love and fear. You can create something from love, seeing that your creation will benefit the world in some way, outside of narrow personal interests. Or you can create something out of fear because you believe that there is something that needs to be controlled, contained, or eradicated.

Schooling started as an idea born of fear, not love. The men who invented modern schooling and created the laws that made attendance at school compulsory wanted to control the "under-class" of people who they feared had the potential to destroy society with their evil ways.

Forced government schooling was invented by men who shared the beliefs of scientific materialism and reductionism, humanism, and socialism. These men believed that, as superior self-chosen elites, they had a responsibility to engineer society in a way that would ensure world order and peace. They believed in the superiority of centralized government institutions run by an elite and distrusted the ingenuity and compassion of individuals and free associations.

Ironically, Horace Mann was largely responsible for getting the first state schools legislated in Massachusetts. He travelled the state giving impassioned speeches saying that parents are not capable of educating their children. Ironically, he chose to homeschool his three sons. This hypocrisy is continued today by the wealthy who could afford to move into the best public school districts but opt for private school for their children instead.

What we see in the worldview of the men who invented public schooling is an impenetrable belief that man, by using science (and social science) could conquer nature and control the minds of individuals. As products of the Enlightenment, they believed in scientific materialism and reductionism. The inventors of school believed that humans were merely soulless animals who could be controlled by social conditioning and psychological techniques. In the 20th Century, school reformers added behavioral psychology and operant conditioning into the classrooms to exert further control over children.

Because the men who invented school viewed people and the world as empty machines, they had no ethical qualms about using schooling to control people. They were the superior self-chosen elites who thought they had the right to redesign society based on their belief systems. They were Religious Humanists and Socialists who did not believe in God or any higher intelligence. They sought to design a society without God.

John Dewey, the father of modern schooling, and a devout socialist who was admired by Soviet revolutionary Leon Trotsky wrote: "The mere absorbing of facts and truths is so exclusively individual an affair that it tends very naturally to pass into selfishness. There is no obvious social motive for the acquirement of mere learning, there is no clear social gain in success thereat." [10]

Again, school was never intended to be an institution that promotes individual learning or well-being, which is why the inventors of school and the wealthy in our current society kept their children out of public school.

President Woodrow Wilson said this in 1909 when he was President of Princeton College:

> *Let us go back and distinguish between the two things that we want to do; for we want to do two things in modern society. We want one class of persons to have a liberal education, and* **we want another class of persons, a very much larger class, of necessity, in every society, to forego the privileges of a liberal education and fit themselves to perform specific difficult manual tasks.** *You cannot train them for both in the time that you have at your disposal... We are either trying to make liberally-educated persons out of them, or we are trying to make skillful servants of society along mechanical lines, or else we do not know what we are trying to do.*

School was designed as an institution to deprive the majority of people of a liberal education and instead force them to endure a program of character reform that would turn them into manual laborers. It was designed to hobble minds so that they wouldn't rebel against inhumane working conditions or the coming totalitarian socialist society.

How do you go about hobbling a mind? Memorization and repetition is the most efficient method of impeding conceptual intellectual development. As we will see in the coming pages, this form of teaching was borrowed from schools in India where drill instruction was used with the lower castes to ensure that they remained ignorant.

Whole-word instruction, which is a system of memorization and drill, has been the primary method of teaching reading in public schools since the mid 1900s. Even though research shows that it results in illiteracy, it is still the primary method of reading instruction. High illiteracy rates in America is the results. Only 13.5% of 15-year olds in America can distinguish between fact and opinion. Remember that before schooling was forced into society, literacy rates were above 90%.

In the 1900s, techniques from behavioral psychology, including operant conditioning, were introduced into public schools in the United States. This operant conditioning has found a great tool in the computer-based technology, which is flooding into schools today, as tech startups see huge profit opportunities. Student behavior, emotional responses, and attitudes are being tracked and controlled.

Schooling is an institution that is designed to create ignorant, fearful, obedient, docile people. It has nothing to do with learning or education except that it hides under the banner of education. I challenge you to go into any school board meeting in America. What you will see discussed is funding and test scores. There will be no mention or thought of student learning or well-being.

To force children to go to school where their minds are numbed by boring, irrelevant, and biased curriculum is unconstitutional. It teaches them to hate learning. Depriving children from being in nature results in their not valuing the earth and life. Pretending that they don't have souls and are not connected to a universal intelligence that many people call God results in anxiety, depression, apathy, suicide, and out-of-control consumerism as people try to buy their way to security.

Separating children from society and their community until they are 18 tells them that they have no true value to society. Thomas Edison, who was taken out of school after his teacher called him "addled" was homeschooled by his mother so that he could reach his full potential. He learned by reading books and avoided math altogether because he disliked it. He famously said, "I can always hire a mathematician, but they can't hire me." Edison worked on a night train selling candy and newspapers when he was 13. That was natural.

Adolescence didn't used to exist in America until the 1930s when school administrators noticed that most people were leaving school after their elementary years to go to work. So, they invented middle school and high school to keep kids in school longer. They extended the compulsory schooling laws. School's creep happened slowly and insidiously.

Trying to reform schools so that they educate people is impossible because the very design of school is designed to impede learning and the development of self-agency so that people can be controlled. Read that again. Designed to impede the development of self-agency. The wealthy and powerful in this country still don't send their children to public school.

Educating yourself is a human right that should be protected in a democracy that was formed on the principles of political equality. People don't see this as a right because they mistakenly think that schooling is education. They are two extremely different endeavors. Schooling, because it impairs our ability to think and denies the infinite intelligence within all people, leads to a society of apathetic, confused, depressed, and anxious people who are all out for number one. School produces insecure, dependent, illiterate young people because that is what it is designed to do.

The Religion of Schooling

*"...without long-term confinement of
children to great warehouses, the amount of
isolation and mind-control needed to
successfully introduce civil religion through
schooling just wasn't available."*
- John Taylor Gatto

The first attempt at schooling that would look similar to today's school began during the Protestant reformation in the 16th and 17th Centuries. Protestant belief was that you needed to be able to read the Bible to get the word of God directly otherwise you would go to hell. The early schools had three intentions: read the Bible, believe the Bible, and be obedient.

The school evangelizers of the 19th Century replaced obedience to God with Obedience to the State as the nation-state emerged as the locus of power. The men who succeeded in expanding modern schooling in the 20th Century were Religious Humanists who wanted to replace religious instruction with secular instruction.

Schooling today propagates a religion called humanism (aka atheism). What is Humanism? Humanism is a progressive philosophy of life that, without theism or other supernatural beliefs, affirms our ability and responsibility to lead ethical lives of personal fulfillment that aspire to the greater good.[11] – American Humanist Association

John Dewey, the father of modern schooling, was a self-proclaimed religious humanist who worked with his contemporaries to create a new religion based on the worldview of humanism. The primary focus of Secular Humanism is to exclude God or any higher power or creative force from the potential answers in life. Dewey said his goal was to create a humanist utopia and that the teacher is the prophet who will usher in this new world order of Man as God.

Dewey was one of 34 signers of the Humanist Manifesto I of 1933[12]. Important elements from this Manifesto include:

"Religious humanists regard the universe as self-existing and not created."

"Humanism asserts that the nature of the universe depicted by modern science makes unacceptable any supernatural or cosmic guarantees of human values."

"The distinction between the sacred and the secular can no longer be maintained."

"Without theism or supernatural beliefs" is also a way of saying atheist. I firmly believe in the right for every individual to worship the God of their understanding, including believing there is no God.

America was founded as a Christian country based on religious freedom and tolerance. Literacy was a primary goal for all citizens so that they could participate in the democratic process and read the bible. All religious beliefs and practices were and are welcome in the United States. Religious freedom does exist in the United States.

In the United States today, 70.6% of people describe themselves as Christian, 1.9% Jewish, 0.9% Buddhist, 0.7% Muslim, 0.7% Hindu, 3.1% atheist, 4% agnostic, and 15.8% "nothing in particular". I'm not sure which bucket Humanism fits into, but probably atheist or agnostic. So, it is interesting that the religion implicitly practiced in public school is Humanism and most people don't know this. They assume that school is areligious. It is not.

In 2014, the American Humanist Association claimed humanism is a religion and sued the United States to allow an inmate to create a humanist group in prison. Humanists won the motion in a U.S. District Court in Portland, Oregon.[13] "The court finds that Secular Humanism is a religion for Establishment Clause purposes.". The court ruled that humanism should be treated as "religion" for purposes of the Equal Protection Clause, which prohibits religious discrimination.

I did my undergrad studies at the University of Virginia, founded by Thomas Jefferson. During freshman orientation, we were told that Thomas Jefferson's proudest achievement was the 1786 Virginia Statute for Religious Freedom. The separation of church and state as codified in the U.S. Constitution 1st Amendment is extremely important to protecting an individual's religious freedom.

> *Congress shall make no law respecting an establishment of religion, or prohibiting the free exercise thereof; or abridging the freedom of speech, or of the press; or the right of the people peaceably to assemble, and to petition the Government for a redress of grievances.*

I am not arguing for including religion in schools. The religion of humanism is already being implicitly taught in schools. Humanism was defined by the United States as a religion. This religion has been taught in public schools for the past 150+ years.

What is the effect of schools teaching humanism on individuals and society? One effect is that generations of individuals believe that they are alone in a cold, uncaring universe. Another is that scientific advances in quantum physics and biology and consciousness studies are systematically excluded from K–12 curriculum.

What is important is for parents, educators, and educational reformers to understand that the worldview that is built into the school system is indeed religious.

> *If humanism were right in declaring that man is born to be happy, he would not be born to die. Since his body is doomed to die, his task on earth evidently must be of a more spiritual nature. It cannot be unrestrained enjoyment of everyday life. It cannot be the search for the best ways to obtain material goods and then cheerfully get the most out of them. It has to be the fulfillment of a permanent, earnest duty so that one's life journey may become an experience of moral growth, so that one may leave life a better human being than one started it. - Aleksandr Solzhenitsyn*

State Schools Were Actively Opposed by Americans

Ellwood Cubberley, one of the nation's first experts in school administration, helped create one of the first schools of education at Stanford and legitimized "education" as a field of study. Cubberley tells us, "The history of compulsory-attendance legislation in the states has been much the same everywhere, and everywhere laws have been enacted only after overcoming strenuous opposition."

The coercion required to keep children's butts in their seats as teachers march them through boring, standardized curriculum breaks their spirits. It is breaking the spirits of teachers too.

> *Very simply, the extension and reform of education in the mid-nineteenth century were not a potpourri of democracy, rationalism and humanitarianism...we must face the painful fact that this country has never, on any large scale, known vital urban schools, ones which embrace and are embraced by the mass of the community, which formulate their goals in terms of the joy of the individual instead of the fear of social dynamite or the imperatives of economic growth. - Michael Katz*

Schooling is a terrible misuse of government power. Government schools are, for some children, the safest place for them to be. I don't think dismantling schools today is the answer for all children. And let's be honest about what schooling really is. Schooling is a completely made-up, unnatural way of trying to force children comply to a strange set of rules.

Schooling continues because there are state laws that make it illegal not to school your child. The force of government keeps it in place. Compulsory schooling hides under the banner of improving people and society even though it continues to produce ignorant, illiterate people and research shows that schooling perpetuates socio-economic inequality.

What Keeps Schooling Frozen in Place?

Schooling occupies a central position in American society. The shared social belief is that schooling is good for everyone and necessary for democracy and economic equality. Yet, everyone admits that the school system is broken, and parents still support public school. Why is this? Most adults cannot conceive of their lives functioning if their children aren't being cared for by the institution of school. Rational irrationality, confirmation bias, and motivated ignorance help explain why schooling is still supported.

Economist Bryan Caplan's concept of "rational irrationality" helps to explain this phenomenon. If you believe that you cannot change a situation (schooling), you will not accept evidence that refutes your cherished belief (kids hate school and aren't learning much) because the emotional cost is too high. Most people do not think that they personally can do anything about the school system, so they refute any evidence that shows how damaging it is to kids.

If someone raises an objection to government schooling or proposes an alternative, school supporters will raise the question of what the objector has to gain and question the person's motives. School supporters will also require impossibly high standards for proposed education alternatives while relaxing the standard for research supporting government schooling.

In addition, confirmation bias will lead people to focus on one amazing teacher or the one child that "seems to" love school. I have always been curious why a parent's perspective is often so different than their child's own experience of school. Many children have told my daughters over the years that they dislike school and wish they could homeschool too. When I speak with the children's mothers, they universally tell me that their child likes school and their school is the best in the community.

Motivated ignorance is when we choose not to know more, we actively choose not to understand. We have developed a conception of the world and willfully remain ignorant to avoid cognitive dissonance which occurs when we hold two opposing ideas in our minds. Motivated ignorance makes us more confident in our belief systems and less likely to consider facts that contradict our beliefs.

Belief is deeply psychological and the one of the best ways to change people's minds is the power of a friend who shares the same beliefs but sees an issue differently. I hope to be your friend on this journey, guiding you to discover what is true for you and your family.

Schooling is Now a Big Business with Grim Results

Schooling in the United States is a $1.3 trillion industry. $1,350,000,000,000. There are a lot of companies making a lot of money – including textbook manufacturers, standardized testing companies, and EdTech startups.

Schooling advocates have powerful lobbying interests that keep schooling funded and prevent alternatives from emerging. Schooling is an education monopoly.

$13,440 is spent per student for public K–12 school each year on average for a total of $680 billion every year. Americans spent $80 billion just on back-to-school purchases in 2019. Philanthropy to support public education is over $60 billion a year.

There are 50.8 million youth in public elementary, middle, and high schools. There were 19.9 million students attending a college or university in fall 2019.

The U.S. Department of Education website states its mission: "Our mission is to promote student achievement and preparation for global competitiveness by fostering educational excellence and ensuring equal access. "And yet… In 2019, Peggy Carr, Associate Commissioner of the National Center for Education Statistics said, "Over the past decade, there has been no progress in either mathematics or reading performance, and the lowest-performing students are doing worse."

The results of public schooling are shockingly grim, evidenced by the high illiteracy rates among 15-year olds[14], college graduates[15], and adults[16]; lack of engagement[17]; student boredom[18]; skyrocketing anxiety, depression, and suicide; continued teacher turnover, and widespread ignorance of fundamental knowledge.

A study of the literacy of college students found that:"More than 75 percent of students at two-year colleges and more than 50 percent of students at four-year colleges do not score at the proficient level of literacy. This means that they lack the skills to perform complex literacy tasks, such as comparing credit card offers with different interest rates or summarizing the arguments of newspaper editorials."[19]

In addition, 45% of people with student loans don't think college was worth it, 36% of college graduates had no cognitive gains after 4 years of college, and 70% of graduates from half of U.S. colleges make no more than high school graduates, college tuition has risen 1200% since 1978, and the average college grad has $30,000 in student debt with monthly payments of $393. Young people are bored, anxious, depressed, not learning much, and college becomes indentured servitude for many people.

Distracting Us with Standards and Testing

In 1965, the Elementary and Secondary School Act (ESEA) was passed as part of President Lyndon B. Johnson's Great Society program. Under Title I funds, it offered more than $1 billion in aid to help schools educate disadvantaged students.[20] Its effect was to put national standards and testing in place and secure the federal government's position in schooling for the first time.

The No Child Left Behind (NCLB) Act passed in 2002 was the first overhaul of ESEA and increased the role of the federal government in holding K-12 schools responsible for academic progress of students, especially subgroups of English language learners, special education students, and poor and minority children. Under this law, schools must test children in reading and math in grades 3 through 8 and once in high school.

The Every Student Succeeds Act (ESSA) was passed in 2015 and was a reauthorization of ESEA. It provided waivers to opt out of NCLB for school districts who could put in their own plans for student success.

What is clear is that almost 55 years of federal education policy has not resulted in student success in reading and math. "Over the past decade, there has been no progress in either mathematics or reading performance, and the lowest-performing students are doing worse," said Peggy Carr, the associate commissioner of the National Center for Education Statistics, which administers the NAEP. "In fact, over the long term in reading, the lowest-performing students—those readers who struggle the most—have made no progress from the first NAEP administration almost 30 years ago."[21]

What has this focus on national standards and testing done for students and teachers? Teachers who enter schooling because they love a subject or love kids, judge themselves harshly when the kids are not engaged or acting out. Often, they feel like it is a personal failure, or they see the inertia in the system and leave. More than 41% of teachers leave the profession within five years of starting.[22]

EdTech is the Nail in the Coffin

*A massive effort is underway to link centrally
organized control of jobs with centrally
organized administration of schooling. This
would be an American equivalent of the
Chinese "Dangan" — linking a personal file
begun in kindergarten (recording academic
performance, attitudes, behavioral
characteristics, medical records, and other
personal data) with all work opportunities. -
John Taylor Gatto*

Many people have written about the problems with school. John
Taylor Gatto did copious research to share the real history of
schooling. Peter Gray has shown us that we are designed to play and
explore and that is how we learn best. Kirsten Olsen set out to
determine how school helped successful people get to where they
were in life and realized that school wounded every single person
she talked to in multiple emotional and psychological ways. People
succeeded in spite of schooling.

The reason that this issue is so pressing now is that, with the
advances in technology, especially artificial intelligence and big data,
schooling becomes an ever more powerful and dangerous weapon.

With the rise of data science, tech entrepreneurs are rushing in
to get a piece of the $1.35 trillion pie. Because they don't
understand how learning happens and how humans are driven to
learn by personal curiosity, their solutions are misguided and
potentially dangerous.

I aim to show you how school was designed to create illiterate,
insecure, dependent people who discount their own inner lives and
spiritual dimensions and have a casual disregard for life.

Before we go there, look at this foreshadowing of what is to
come if we don't break the trance of schooling. Personalized
Learning" and "Learner-Centered" projects are being used as a
banner for big brother tracking and surveillance.

I remember telling my young daughter that it didn't matter how old you were when you learned to read because nobody would know. A friend of mine is a teacher who specializes in gifted education. She told me that gifted students either learn to read early (by age 4) or late (around age 12).

Using Computer Algorithms to Invade the Privacy of Mind

Let's look at BrainCo that came out of Harvard and NASA. BrainCo's Focus Edu solution puts EEG headbands called LUCY on students to track their level of attention. The headband system was first introduced in China because it was determined there would be less pushback from parents. However, when pictures like the one below were circulated on social media in China, the program was suspended.

I showed this picture to my daughter who tried public schooling. She was terrified! She said, "When I was bored in school and daydreaming, I remember thinking, "At least the teacher cannot read my mind."

This technology allows teachers and administrators to force kids to pay attention. It is the most invasive technology I have seen. Why do the creators of Lucy think this is okay?

Image from BrainCo website[23]

Max Newton, the scientist who created the LUCY algorithm says: "One thing we're hoping to use this for is to detect users' interest," Newton says. "There's a subjective component people already experience. We want to make it visible and put a number on it so people can learn more about what's going on in their brains."

From the BrainCo website:

> "BrainCo's Focus EDU is a classroom system that lets the teacher monitor a class's attention level in real time, as an average or as a "heat map" of the classroom, and it generates an after-class report on the group as a whole, as well as individual students' attention levels.
>
> An LED light on the front of each student's headband can indicate one of three attention levels, although Newton says the feature is generally turned off during class time. "You don't want to distract students with their friends' headband colors."

The classroom version gives teachers overall student attention reports to see what's getting kids' attention, where they're getting lost, and even whether they're relaxed during breaks. Individual student reports let them see who's having trouble paying attention and when.

Do you believe that brains are just like computers and that they can be upgraded with technology? If so, then you might think putting LUCY in classrooms and homes so that teachers and parents can control children's' subjective experience of life is okay.

If you understand that a person's subjective experience of life is private and should not be quantified, made public, and tracked, then you will be alarmed by this EEG technology that has been unleashed with a computer algorithm. If you further understand that we live in the experience of our thinking as we will explore later, you will be terrified by this technology.

The End of Privacy

Wall-mounted camera monitors a classroom at AltSchool's former location.[24]

AltSchool was created by former Google executive, Max Ventilla, to reinvent school. The startup got $175 million in venture capital to create micro-schools and a new learning management system that replaces teachers with playlists and video surveillance. In 2017, AltSchool closed its micro-schools to focus on developing the platform and selling it to public schools and rebranded itself "Altitude Learning". Despite complaints from parents whose children attended the micro-schools before they were shuttered, Altitude promises learner-centered schooling.

One parent whose children attended AltSchool microschools said to Business Insider: "We knew that [Ventilla] was trying to create software that would improve the educational system," a parent of a former AltSchool student said. But, she added, "How can you bring personalized learning to other schools when it's failing miserably at the school you're running?"[25]

Altitude is now selling this "learner-centered" playlist system to school districts complete with data tracking, assessments, and video monitors. With a widespread teacher shortage, can you see school districts buying this technology even though many children at the AltSchool microschool were struggling to learn anything with this approach?

Replacing curriculum with curated playlists like those offered by Altitude Learning and the Zuckerberg-backed Summit Learning Platform tracks highly personal data about student's learning activities. More than 100 students from Brooklyn's Secondary School for Journalism walked out of school in 2017, protesting the Summit Learning Platform and saying they weren't learning anything and were concerned about privacy issues.

Below is an excerpt from a letter published in the Washington Post in November 2018:

Unfortunately, we didn't have a good experience using the program, which requires hours of classroom time sitting in front of computers. Not all students would receive computers, the assignments are boring, and it's too easy to pass and even cheat on the assessments. Students feel as if they are not learning anything and that the program isn't preparing them for the Regents exams they need to pass to graduate. Most importantly, the entire program eliminates much of the human interaction, teacher support, and discussion and debate with our peers that we need in order to improve our critical thinking.

Unlike the claims made in your promotional materials, we students find that we are learning very little to nothing. It's severely damaged our education, and that's why we walked out in protest.

Another issue that raises flags to us is all our personal information the Summit program collects without our knowledge or consent. We were never informed about this by Summit or anyone at our school, but recently learned that Summit is collecting our names, student ID numbers, email addresses, our attendance, disability, suspension and expulsion records, our race, gender, ethnicity and socio-economic status, our date of birth, teacher observations of our behavior, our grade promotion or retention status, our test scores and grades, our college admissions, our homework, and our extracurricular activities. Summit also says on its website that they plan to track us after graduation through college and beyond. Summit collects too much of our personal information and discloses this to 19 other corporations.

What gives you this right, and why weren't we asked about this before you and Summit invaded our privacy in this way?[26]

In the wake of school shooting tragedies, a school surveillance industry has sprouted up offering to monitor students' online activity including personal emails and social media. While the intention may be good, does anybody see how this is a violation of the 4th Amendment of the U.S. Constitution?

The 4th Amendment:
The right of the people to be secure in their persons, houses, papers, and effects, against unreasonable searches and seizures, shall not be violated, and no warrants shall issue, but upon probable cause, supported by oath or affirmation, and particularly describing the place to be searched, and the persons or things to be seized.

Youth are living in the legacy of having no personal rights once they enter the school building. More than 60 school districts have spent over $1m on separate monitoring technology to track what their students were saying on public social media accounts.[27]

A study by Carnegie Mellon University found that, "Beyond complying with federal and state-level requirements, EdTech startups do not prioritize student data protections, as compared to customer acquisition and product development in their first five years." and "Concerns about complying with privacy regulation and guidance do not seem to inhibit innovation at EdTech startups."[28]

Perhaps the vision of the men who invented school to completely redesign society is coming to fruition at the feet of generations of schooled and dis-spirited people. I understand that at the core of every human is an unbreakable spirit. We cannot let schooling, technology, and surveillance break our connection to this spirit.

Homeschooling Under Attack

Homeschooling continues to be under attack around the world. The National Education Association, that claims to have 3.2 million teachers as members, states in its 2018-19 Resolutions:

> *The National Education Association believes that home schooling programs based on parental choice cannot provide the student with a comprehensive education experience. When home schooling occurs, students enrolled must meet all state curricular requirements, including the taking and passing of assessments to ensure adequate academic progress.*
>
> *Home schooling should be limited to the children of the immediate family, with all expenses being borne by the parents/guardians. Instruction should be by persons who are licensed by the appropriate state education licensure agency, and a curriculum approved by the state department of education should be used.*
>
> *The Association also believes that home-schooled students should not participate in any extracurricular activities in the public schools.*

So, even though public schools are ineffective at teaching reading, math, and civics, the NEA believes that parents cannot provide a "comprehensive education experience". The Homeschool Legal Defense Association has statistics on the academic success of homeschoolers.

A study "by Dr. Lawrence Rudner of 20,760 homeschooled students found the homeschoolers who have homeschooled all their school aged years had the highest academic achievement. This was especially apparent in the higher grades."

Another important finding of Strengths of Their Own was that the race of the student does not make any difference. There was no significant difference between minority and white homeschooled students.

These findings show that when parents, regardless of race, commit themselves to make the necessary sacrifices and tutor their children at home, almost all obstacles present in other school systems disappear.

In *Strengths of Their Own*, Dr. Ray found the average cost per homeschool student is $546 while the average cost per public school student is $5,325. Dr Ray says, "The message is loud and clear. More money does not mean a better education. There is no positive correlation between money spent on education and student performance. Public school advocates could refocus their emphasis if they learned this lesson. Loving and caring parents are what matters. Money can never replace simple, hard work."

PART 3: How Humans Operate & Learn

The Invitation

As human beings we must look closely at the
relationship between our spiritual nature and
our psychological nature. Here we will find the
answers we seek to change the deplorable state
of the world. - Sydney Banks, The Missing Link

Your life is about to get a whole lot easier and better. 99.9% of what you've been told about life is wrong. When you see how simple life really is, you will wonder why you weren't taught this in Kindergarten.

After guiding many children and parents on their soul-directed living and learning paths, I have come to understand education as a spiritual practice. This has nothing to do with religion. It is based on the spiritual truths that operate in the background of our lives whether or not we are religious.

When we educate to preserve children's innate wholeness, wisdom and wellbeing, young people will unleash their unlimited capacity to innovate. They can evolve the world and society in a positive direction through their insights.

Before we explore how life really works, it's helpful to understand the difference between an idea and a principle. Principles are fundamental truths that do not have any exceptions.

One principle you are familiar with is gravity. Gravity is at work in your life whether you acknowledge it or not. If you drop your coffee mug it will fall to the ground. Mathematics is based on universal principles. 2+2=4. Even if you don't know how to add, this principle always works. There are three universal principles we can use to explain the human experience. They function in the background of our life, like gravity and mathematics, whether we recognize them or not. If you choose to understand how they work, your life will get a whole lot simpler.

A Fresh Look at Life

When you understand how your human system operates and how you create your reality moment-by-moment through your thinking, life gets a lot easier and better.

Let's talk about fear. What is fear? Does it really protect you from danger? The only time that fear is useful is when your life is in danger - there is a snake on the path, and you freeze. You bump into a bear in the woods and flee. You're jogging down the path and encounter an angry poodle and fight it off. Fight, flight, freeze. That is what the surge of adrenaline produced by an acute stab of fear does for us.

> *Throughout time, humankind has sought peace and safety by trying to out-guess the unknown. We have tried to anticipate and prepare for the unexpected and the apparitions of our minds. In an age of 24-hour cable news, when we can stay glued to the latest terrorist attack or natural disaster, the next epidemic, and what the pundits tell us we should be afraid of, our efforts to control the unknown and thus keep ourselves safe have led to a collective as well as a personal sensation of fear. We have become addicted to fear. – Joseph Bailey, Fearproof Your Life*

Chronic fear is a different thing. Fear, and the fear-based emotions anxiety, stress, and worry are not your friends. We've been trained to think that we are being responsible adults when we worry. So, we worry about the future. We worry about our kids, the economy, our health, the environment, and terrorist attacks. We are a very worried society.

We are also an anxious society. Do you know who in our society is the most worried? Teenagers! The reason they are worried... fear about personal achievement (or lack of it) in school and their future success in life.

We are literally worrying ourselves to death. There is a high correlation between stress and sickness. Dr. Bruce Lipton estimates that 90% of disease is caused by stress. Rates of depression and suicide are higher now than they were during WWII - a time in human history of complete social and economic upheaval. If events in the outside world really caused mental dis-ease, wouldn't we have seen more at that time?

Let's explore what fear is and how you can fear-proof your Self.

LIE: *Your Thoughts are True*

We are held captive by our thoughts, believing that they are all true. They feel true because they produce strong emotions and sensations. I was trained to believe that I am my intellect and to believe all of my thoughts. My self-worth became intricately connected to grades, ranking, titles, and achievement.

You live 100% in the experience of your thinking. It is actually all you can ever experience. Do not believe the endless stream of worries about the future or regrets of the past. Over 70% of everyone's thoughts are negative. It's like you have a toxic iPod playing in your brain all the time. Don't believe it.

LIE: *Worry and Anxiety = Responsible.*

Here is how your beautiful, elegant operating system works: you have an experience, you think about it, your conditioned thought patterns make it mean something (good or bad) and then you have emotions. Most of the time, this happens so quickly, we are unaware of the process. We just suddenly have strong emotions and then we say, "what happened?" meaning what happened in the outside world to make me feel this way?

You cannot control your thoughts and they don't need to control you. Watch your thoughts come and go. Your free will is your ability to choose which thoughts you give life to. Most of us have an experience, thinking comes up about it which creates a feeling. Then, we take that feeling and project it onto the experience.

Media companies and marketers manipulate us

To be a responsible citizen in today's world, you've been trained to plug into the media to stay informed. Little do you know that you are being fed a very distorted view of reality. 6 multinational companies own almost all of the media: the internet, cable, TV, and print media and they have an agenda. It's crazy to think that Disney owns the History Channel and Time Warner owns Gaia.

Mass media and social media companies feed you a steady diet of fear-porn.

The media uses highly biased emotionally charged words like "operative" and "heart-wrenching" combined with vague words like "presumed" and "allegedly" to keep you both fearful and confused. So, if we plug into a bad news story and it's gloomy, end of the world stuff, we are conditioned to worry. We start having fearful thoughts. We start worrying and feel fear, anxiety, and upset.

As an informed citizen, you need to understand that the media is constructing a highly strategic narrative about the world and your place in it. When you can see the narrative for what it is, you cannot be manipulated.

In the 1950s, companies started hiring behavioral psychologists to do advertising campaigns that would make people want to buy their products. Their task was to create artificial demand for a product that people didn't need yet. Take Wonder Bread for example. How did companies get women to buy bread instead of making it themselves? They bleached it! They found that white fluffy bread was psychologically appealing to women. How did the razor companies get us to buy razors? By convincing women that leg hair was unsightly.

To extend it to your childhood, how did teachers get you to sit still and pay attention to boring subjects in school and compete in the endless game of information processing? Through operant conditioning that the behavioral psychologist brought into schooling. Rewards (gold stars, good grades, high GPA, honor roll, teacher approval) and punishments (bad grades, flipped cards, shame and embarrassment, being ignored by the teacher) are all ways to psychologically manipulate you.

And I'm not trying to blame or demonize teachers. They too are trapped in the artificial system of information processing when they would rather be waking kids up to their inner genius. But we need to delve a bit deeper into where your emotions are coming from. Is it the news story? The argument you just had with a co-worker? The guy that cut you off in traffic?

LIE: You are powerless

Society trains us to believe that there is a world outside of us and we are just reacting to it. The best we can hope to do is notice our reactions and work hard to change them to positive ones. The outside, objective world has the power. We don't.

When another person says or does something that you don't like, you believe that experience creates your emotions.

We are conditioned to analyze everything with our logical brains. We are taught to believe every thought that pops into our head. "Wow, they said I was lazy. That makes me mad!"

We live in our thinking-emotional reality. We do not live in the emotion of our experiences. It is what we THINK about our experiences that result in our emotions. Two people can have the exact same experience and view it differently, tell different stories about it, and have different emotions.

LIE: You are Alone in a Cold, Uncaring World

We have been trained to see the world through a materialist lens. In this worldview, the only thing that is real is physical matter. You are a separate block of physical matter that is alone in a cold, uncaring dead universe of other unintelligent matter. Millions of years of evolution produced a brain that gave you consciousness. When you die, your separate self and consciousness are no more. So, you do your best to survive in this cold, competitive, uncaring world. You try to make some money, take care of your family, look out for #1, and hope for the best.

LIE: *You are Not Enough*

Growing up, there is always something that you're not naturally good at. You start believing that you are somehow lacking and need to fix yourself. It becomes your shameful secret. You think if you can just get enough money or followers or stuff, you will be okay. That's why every YouTuber and digital marketing guru talks about the Imposter Syndrome. Apparently, even Facebook COO Sheryl Sandberg has imposter syndrome[29].

School trains us to compare ourselves to others in the game of who can process the most information wins. School forced us to focus on our weaknesses so that we could get straight As, a high GPA, get into an elite college, and then hope there was a job waiting for us so that we could pay off student loan debt. The result is that we all judge ourselves as unworthy. This training of generations has led to an epidemic of anxiety, depression, hostility, fear, and loneliness.

We need to break the cultural trance of fear and we do it one person at a time. I invite you to learn how your beautifully designed human operating system really works. It's quite magical!

TRUTH: *you are a powerful energetic being, not a separate block of physical matter*

Science is currently engaged in a shift that is equal in importance to the Copernican revolution. When science is freed from the myths of materialism, you find that consciousness is primary and human thought is the most powerful creative force on the planet.

There is a universal intelligence behind all life. It is an intelligent energy that grows babies, opens roses, and flows through all humans. It is far more powerful than our intellect. Our brains are tools of this universal intelligence, not its master.

How can you possibly know that it exists? Because it comes to you in moments when you are calm and relaxed, and you have a sudden insight or ah-ha moment. That's why so many people have great ideas in the shower or when walking the dog.

Quantum physicists and biologists have discovered something amazing about life. Life requires 3 things: energy, matter, and information. With the discovery of the human genome, they found that encoded in the DNA of all living things is information. Because of the advances in digital information and AI, they now know that this information cannot be random and cannot have emerged gradually through natural selection. There just wasn't enough time for this to happen.

So, the million-dollar question: where did the genetic information in all living things come from? There must be an intelligent energy that is powering all life. Let's face it, scientists have come up with some pretty cool technology that has made our lives infinitely more interesting and have protected us from the elements of nature. But no human has been able to create life. So, how does life happen? If humans can't create it, aren't we playing God when we try to control it?

Anita Moorjani said in one of her podcasts, that when she crossed over to the other side during her near-death experience, she saw that the part of us that resides in our bodies is only 20% of us. She urges us to connect with and love the other 80% of us that we cannot see.

TRUTH: *The only thing that exists is the eternal NOW*

All of our thinking is about the past or the future. When you focus your attention on the present moment, you are wisdom. You can only be where your feet are. The NOW is the only thing that exists. The past only exists in your thinking – in your memories. The past is not real. The future is not real. And no amount of worrying or planning will control its outcome.

There are lots of ways to get present, be mindful, and be where your feet are including: meditation, walks in nature, music, laughter, breathing.

TRUTH: *Your feelings and sensations are your GPS*

Your emotions are a psychological compass that tells you the state of your thinking. Nothing more. Nothing Less.

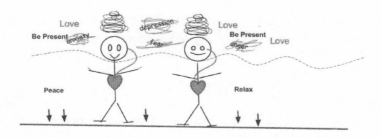

Relax into your heart space. Under your thinking, beliefs, and assumptions... you are PURE LOVE. Our true essence is LOVE. Not romantic love, but unconditional love of all that is.

I was told to ignore or mistrust emotions—they are irrational. I struggled to make sense of the ongoing battle between my head and my heart. To make decisions, I'd make a logical pros and cons list.

I now understand that I am love. I don't need to look outside of myself for something that I already am. I can go into the world needing nothing, ready to connect through love. To experience love as your true essence, it can be as simple as breathing into your heart space and feeling the warmth and love that is there.

TRUTH: *Your body is intelligent*

Our body has natural intelligence and is trying to communicate with us every second. Every cell of your body is intelligent. Relax into your body. Connect with the energy and intelligence behind all life.

I was trained to see my body as just a vehicle for my brain. 13+ years being forced to sit still and use your intellect for rote memorization has disconnected you from a body that wanted to be outside, run, play, move.

Medical professionals apply band-aids to any symptoms of disease that popped up. I now understand that my body is continually sending me messages to let me know if I am on the best path for my highest good. Am I really following my true calling and hearing the whispers of my soul? Begin to move mindfully again. Do a body scan daily. Yoga, Tai Chi, Qi Gong, Dance, or other somatic practices can re-connect you with the intelligence of your body.

TRUTH: *Your intuition/inner knowing guides you*

You are always guided moment by moment to action that serves your highest Self. Our intuition/inner wisdom is a quiet whisper that we can hear when we take time to be quiet. You were born with this innate intelligence until it was conditioned out of you. I know what my intuition feels like in my body. YES is light, expansive, and full of energy. NO is heavy and I energetically shrink. You do not *have* wisdom. You *are* wisdom. Life is living you as it grows your fingernails, breathes your lungs, and beats your heart.

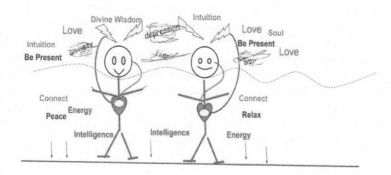

TRUTH: *You are part of the greater whole*

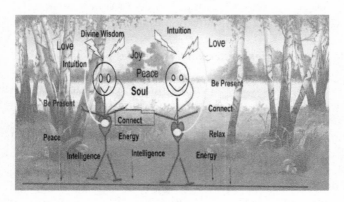

We are trained to see nature as something to be tamed and conquered. It is unpredictable and random. Human technology can conquer it. How well is that working? Here's a better view of life and self from science, common sense, and direct experience.

In nature, we see the abundance, perfection, and oneness of all life. Experience your Self connected to the Oneness of life. Reject all thoughts and fears that you are separate, alone, or unsupported. Nature beckons to you to come and experience your connection to life. The gentle breeze, warm sun, cool rain, icy winds, call of the birds, buzzing of insects, kisses from your dog are all invitations to join in the majesty and beauty of this earth.

> *The major problems in the world are the*
> *result of the difference between how nature*
> *works and the way people think*
> — *Gregory Bateson*

Who Are You?

> As woo-woo as it may sound, you are not a
> physical body as much as you are an energetic
> being vibrating in the universe at a unique
> frequency that distinguishes your self-identity
> from the space and form around you. The fabric
> of your body is a veritable universe of atoms
> that knit together your biochemistry and cell
> biology. Mind bending as it is, only 0.01% of
> that fabric is solid (protons, neutrons, electrons)
> and the other 99.99% of your atomic makeup is
> actually vacuum space. While there is no
> physical mass in this space, it is far from empty.
> In fact, it is full of the electromagnetic field that
> emanates from your core. - Zach Bush, MD

Wayne Dyer talks about the intelligence and energy behind all life that opens roses and grows our fingernails. The same intelligence that is in everything is created and powers each person. When you look into the eyes of another person, you are seeing that unique, unrepeatable expression of the divine. When you look in the mirror, you are looking at intelligent energy that many people call God expressing as you.

You are alive. You are made of aliveness, an intelligent energy, life itself. Universal Mind is the intelligent energy that powers all life. This is the universal, impersonal intelligence that opens roses, turns acorns into oak trees, grew you from a single cell into a whole person, and powers the amazing operations of your body. Inside of all of us is a boundless, formless, creative energy that cannot be damaged or hurt. Everyone has access to this intelligence. Not just the affluent or lucky.

You are awareness. Consciousness is what allows you to know and perceive. You are pure, impersonal awareness. Within this space of awareness thoughts arise and disappear. A useful metaphor is seeing yourself as the clear blue sky and your thoughts as clouds that move across the sky. We are conditioned to look at the clouds, not the sky.

You think. You are the thinker. You are not your thoughts. You live 100% in the experience and feeling of your thinking. Each of us constructs a Self and a world through our thinking process and then choose moment-by-moment how to live in this thought created reality. When we understand that, we are free. We don't need to take any of our thinking seriously. With this understanding, you cannot be controlled or manipulated by fear-based authorities, systems, or propaganda.

How We Create Reality

If the only thing people learned was not to
be afraid of their experience, that alone would
change the world.– Sydney Banks

We have all been trained to believe that we live in the experience of what is happening around us. Events and other people make us feel certain ways. For example, if someone is upset, we immediately ask them, "What happened?" This perpetuates the mistaken belief that outside experiences create our internal feeling state.

As Bruce Lipton, author of *The Biology of Belief,* tells us, when we think, we are defaulting to our subconscious mind which is just playing other people's programs. Dr. Lipton estimates that 70-80% of these thoughts are negative, disempowering, and self-sabotaging. He estimates that we spend 95% of each day ruminating in thinking. We don't observe our own behavior because we are focused on thinking.

Joseph Bailey, in Fearproof Your Life, describes this as our ego-based thought system that is addicted to fear. He says, "When we only look to our intellectual thought system and those of others, we are trapped by their inherent limitations."

Our psyches are manipulated, and we are conditioned to be N.I.C.E. by society and schooling.

Neurotic – believing your negative thoughts about yourself and the world

Insecure – believing that you are not enough and not okay

Controlling – trying to control the experiences you have in life so that you feel okay

Ego-Tripper – innocently thinking that you are just are just a body carrying a brain and need to achieve your goals before you have permission to love yourself

Our thinking is a system of choices that is limited by what we think we know.

It's like every person is walking around engaging with a negative thought bubble over their heads rather than engaging in the moment-by-moment experience of life. Or that we all have an iPod implanted in our brains running negative tapes over and over.

What fascinates me, and I hope will capture your attention, is that the conditioned thinking that we all default to was given to us by society and schooling.

In my coaching training program, I was taught that our behavior is determined by our moods. And that our stories create our moods. We worked to shift our mood by changing our story or shifting our body posture. The book *You Are What You Say* by Matthew Budd and Larry Rothstein does a good job of explaining a lot of this. It is good but it doesn't go deep enough to the source of creating.

I discovered the missing piece to the puzzle when I was introduced to the work of Sydney Banks, a Scottish mystic, who in 1973 had an enlightenment experience. Sydney Banks shared his understanding of how life works through the Three Principles of *Mind*, *Consciousness*, and **Thought**. These principles existed before the creation of form, before the creation of the physical universe that we know.

Mind is the energy and intelligence behind all life. Many people also call this Universal Mind, Divine Mind, or God. It is the life force that flows through everything. Mind is the source of all ideas and creativity.

Consciousness allows us to be aware of life

Thought is how we experience life. We experience life by our thinking. Thinking is the gift all living beings have been given that allows us to create our realities.

These principles transcend all concepts and religions. So, you don't need to put your religion aside to understand them.

Thinking Your Way Through Life

It may be difficult to believe that you have a spiritual operating system since you have been trained to believe the opposite. Please do not believe my words. Investigate these ideas directly. Explore how you experience life.

We live in the experience of our thinking. We only experience life through our thinking. By placing our attention on something, we notice it. Our thinking makes the experience a reality to us. If we don't notice it or think about it, we do not experience it.

We don't see life the way it is, we see it the way we think it is. Often our thinking-sensing-feeling happens so quickly that it is invisible to us. We notice something in the outside world just feel the sensations in our body and feelings that we give labels to (sad, angry, upset).

> *All emotions are the biochemical result of a*
> *thought or series of thoughts in our brain.*
> *Through the link of our neurotransmitters, our*
> *thoughts, and neuropeptides, we create a*
> *cascade of emotions with each series of*
> *associative thoughts. As such, emotions are a*
> *feedback mechanism informing us of the proper*
> *use of our thinking and behavior.*
> *- Joseph Bailey, Fearproof Your Life, p. 64*

We end up trying to control our experiences so that we feel a certain way. If I have negative thinking that produces negative emotions, I will do lots of things to try and numb my feelings if I believe them to be true.

If I have negative thinking, start to feel negative emotions, and then realize it's all based on a lie (faulty thinking), I can let it pass and quickly come back to center where there is peace and serenity. We all have freedom of mind -- the ability to choose which thoughts we give life to. And we have free will - how we choose to respond to our thinking and what actions we take. We can use thoughts to make our existence heaven on earth or hell.

The Conceptual Brain & The Creative Mind

The mind is more extensive than the brain. –
Rupert Sheldrake

You have been taught that you are a body carrying around a brain. Here's how your brain works: you can only get out of it what you put into it. So, garbage in, garbage out. This is the conceptual brain which is the only part of your thought system that schooling acknowledges.

Schooling is based on filling this conceptual brain with information. Schooling focuses on our computer-like brains and intellect. It neglects and disowns our innate intelligence. And we are taught to misuse the gift of thinking.

Because of this, we are trained to operate on the habitual thought patterns that get ingrained in our intellectual thought systems early in our lives.

Here's how your Creative Mind works: You create a question you want to answer or a problem you want to solve. You investigate, research, and experiment. If you feel lost, confused or overwhelmed, there are powerful questions you can ask your true Self. "What am I not seeing here?" "What is mine to do?" "Are there other questions that I need to ask?"

Then you leave the question or problem alone and relax as you do another activity. Your mind will present you with a fresh idea that emerges from seemingly nowhere.

How does this happen? Because your creative mind is a part of universal mind – the source of all creativity and creation. This is what Carl Jung calls the collective unconscious. You must trust and surrender and be willing to listen to the quiet voice within that guides you gently through life.

The conceptual or analytic brain is extremely valuable. Humans are the only animals who have this gift. But the brain is just a tool of your personal mind. When your personal mind is connected to Universal Mind, you operate from a place of wisdom, not of emotional reactivity.

The challenge is that schooling trains us to ignore our inner voice that is telling us school is boring, tedious, abusive, and unnatural.

Soul-directed learning acknowledges the wisdom of the inner child in you and your children. Psychologist James Hillman, author of The Soul's Code, introduced us to the acorn theory. It views children like acorns. Acorns have everything they need inside to become an oak tree. Children have everything they need inside of themselves to reach their full potential. When they have a desire to do or learn something, it is their soul's inner guidance.

The Non-Mechanical Universe

*Today there is a wide measure of agreement,
which on the physical side of science approaches
almost to unanimity, that the stream of
knowledge is heading towards a non-mechanical
reality; the universe begins to look more like a
great thought than like a great machine. Mind
no longer appears as an accidental intruder into
the realm of matter; we are beginning to suspect
that we ought rather to hail it as a creator and
governor of the realm of matter. — Sir James
Jeans, In The Mysterious Universe*

Newtonian physics is what most of us learn in high school. Most
of us don't learn quantum physics unless we choose this course in
college or university. Well known paradigm shifts in science include
the Copernican revolution in astronomy, the Darwinian theory of
evolution in biology, and the relativity and quantum mechanics
revolutions in the 20th Century.

*For centuries, scientists assumed that
everything can be explained by mechanisms
analogous to clockworks. But over the course of
the 20th century, we've learned that this
common sense assumption is wrong. When the
fabric of reality is examined very closely,
nothing resembling clockworks can be found.
Instead, reality is woven from strange, "holistic"
threads that aren't located precisely in space or
time. Tug on a dangling loose end from this
fabric of reality, and the whole cloth twitches,
instantly, throughout all space and time. - Dean
Radin*

We need to ask why findings in quantum mechanics, quantum biology, and consciousness studies are being excluded from K-12 schooling. The discoveries of quantum mechanics began over a century ago. Is it because it doesn't fit with the religion of humanism that excludes the existence of anything non-material? Perhaps it's because you cannot introduce quantum mechanics without bringing in the debate about the origin of life.

While fossil records do prove that life is old on this planet (~4 billion years old) and has changed over time, there is no scientific evidence of how life first started. The big bang is an intriguing theory with evidence of a field of expanding background radiation. And yet it is just a theory without scientific proof.

What quantum physics is discovering is that there are two worlds – the material and the non-material that are connected. Scientific materialism works well in explaining how the material world works, but it breaks down when trying to explain the non-material.

The Mystery of Consciousness

Contrast materialist dogma with the post-material paradigm that emerges from quantum mechanics postulates that the origin of life is of a mental nature: universal mind or consciousness.

> *The nature of the mind is the most unsolved problem that science cannot deal with. It cannot deal with the fact that we are conscious, and our thoughts and experiences don't seem to be inside your brain. - Rupert Sheldrake*

Quantum physics has demonstrated undeniably that the answer we get in scientific inquiry depends on the question being asked and the person who is observing the experiment.

Our minds are not just inside of our heads. Rupert Sheldrake asks about the Paradox of Self-Consciousness: "If I'm conscious of consciousness, if I'm consciously thinking about thinking, I change the state that I'm targeting because my overall mental state is now different."

Engaging young people in this conversation and debate would be a tremendous educational project. Pretending that science has all of the answers shuts down curiosity and inquiry. Dogmatic assumptions inhibit inquiry and discovery.

> *Dis-spirited schooling has been tested and found fully wanting. I think that's partially because it denies the metaphysical reality recognized by men and women worldwide, today and in every age. - John Taylor Gatto*

These are exciting times. There is a unique opportunity to engage young people in this fascinating debate. Are we just biological machines? Or do we have a soul? Is there a collective consciousness that we share?

Why are children taught the materialistic version of the origin of life? Wouldn't it result in a more intellectually stimulating environment to tell kids the truth that science itself is a continually evolving field and we don't know what we don't know? It would then allow for parents to provide religious education at home, free from the bias of scientific materialism and reductionism.

Of course, this would create a generation of children who would think critically for themselves, and perhaps this is not what the founders of government schools intended. You have been told that consciousness emerged on this planet when human brains became complex enough to be aware of self. It was an evolutionary process you were taught. This is not true. Science has yet to explain the existence of human consciousness or where thinking comes from.

What scientists have discovered through repeatable experiments is that consciousness affects physical outcomes. Many scientists are beginning to suspect that consciousness came first. Then came the physical world of form.

Scientific experiments suggest that there is a non-material field that is affecting the physical world. Experiments conducted on mice that show that parent's experiences and fear responses are inherited by their offspring suggest that "the experiences of a parent, before even conceiving offspring, markedly influence both structure and function in the nervous system of subsequent generations."[30]

> *It is difficult for the matter-of-fact physicist to accept the view that the substratum of everything is of mental character. But no one can deny that mind is the first and most direct thing in our experience, and all else is remote inference.* — Eddington, The Nature of the Physical World

God/Mind/Consciousness is the formless energy that existed before form. All people are animated by this formless energy. It connects us. Perhaps it is light energy, since we are beings of light.

It is one thing to understand that Mind is everything - pure energy - the formlessness, the all-that-is and another to have a direct experience of it. Sydney Banks said that you are looking for a feeling, not an intellectual understanding of the three principles. It is Universal Mind that I feel when I connect with the knowing, non-judgmental presence that I truly am.

Mind is everything that is alive. Everything. Without exception. Because God is not some old man on a cloud that waits for judgment day. If all-that-is can be viewed as an endless ocean, we are all waves on the ocean of life. Connected. One. I experience God when I look into my daughters' eyes, watch a cardinal flying about, see a bright purple sunset, smell the rain, get moved by a beautiful piece of music, and have an ah-ha! moment.

Mind is our life force. We take this formless energy (Mind) and, through our thinking, turn it into all sorts of forms.

Meeting Your True Self

*The mind's knowledge of anything is only as
good as its knowledge of itself. Therefore, there
is no higher knowledge than to know the
nature of the mind.*
-Rupert Spira

I am going to make an artificial distinction that will be
inaccurate but extremely helpful: your human operating system and
your spiritual operating system.

We believe that we are a physical body sitting still and reading
this. That is an illusion. We are on a planet that is moving in
different directions at differing speeds. You are a being of light on a
planet that is spinning around its axis at 1,000 miles per hour, while
the earth orbits the sun at 67,000 MPH, while our Solar System is
orbiting the center of the Milky Way Galaxy at 140 miles per
second and the Milky Way Galaxy is moving toward the center of
our Local Group of galaxies at 25 miles per second and our Local
Group is hurtling through space at 375 miles per second toward the
Virgo Supercluster.

We are unique forms of the formless. What makes each person
different is our spiritual and psychological understanding. There is
nothing impossible. You are made of universal intelligence. You are
a body of light.

Life operates by a set of universal principles. They operate like
gravity and work even if we are not aware of them. We are
different because we operate at different levels of consciousness
which leads us to use the power of thought differently. Think of it
as a spectrum between universal consciousness and human
consciousness. Ideally, we want the spectrum to be very short.
Currently, it is very wide.

We are all perfect spiritual beings who get stuck in faulty,
negative thinking. Our thinking has been polluted by a culture that
values material wealth, competition, fame and fortune. We operate

from a place of personal thinking that is based on insecurity and lack.

> *With the tool of free will, anyone can forge*
> *a personal purpose. Free will allows infinite*
> *numbers of human stories to be written in*
> *which a personal you is the main character. The*
> *sciences, on the other hand, hard or soft, assume*
> *that purpose and free will are hogwash; given*
> *enough data, everything will be seen as*
> *explainable, predetermined, and predictable. –*
> *John Taylor Gatto*

I believe that people, no matter their age or stage, have the right to determine what they think and believe and that it is not the government's right to force people to believe anything. As we have seen, your thinking is the creative force in your life. Schooling has some built in belief systems that I don't think most Americans agree with when they are thoroughly investigated and held up to scrutiny.

> *The ancient religious question of free will*
> *marks the real difference between schooling and*
> *education. Education is conceived in Western*
> *history as a road to knowing yourself, and*
> *through that knowledge, arriving at a further*
> *understanding of community, relationships,*
> *jeopardy, living nature, and inanimate matter.*
> *But none of those things has any particular*
> *meaning until you see what they lead up to,*
> *finally being in full command of the spectacular*
> *gift of free will: a force completely beyond the*
> *power of science to understand.*
> *– John Taylor Gatto*

Your Inner Calling

> *"You possess a kind of inner force that seeks
> to guide you toward your Life's Task— what
> you are meant to accomplish in the time that
> you have to live. In childhood this force was
> clear to you. It directed you toward activities
> and subjects that fit your natural inclinations,
> that sparked a curiosity that was deep and
> primal. In the intervening years, the force tends
> to fade in and out as you listen more to parents
> and peers, to the daily anxieties that wear away
> at you. This can be the source of your
> unhappiness— your lack of connection to who
> you are and what makes you unique. The first
> move toward mastery is always inward—
> learning who you really are and reconnecting
> with that innate force. Knowing it with clarity,
> you will find your way to the proper career path
> and everything else will fall into place. It is
> never too late to start this process."*
> *- Robert Greene, Mastery*

You are not a mechanical widget that came here without a purpose. Dr. Ali Binazir calculated that the odds of you being alive are about 1 in $10^{2,685,00031}$. This is an incredibly small chance. The odds of you being alive are so small, that you have to conclude that you are a miracle.

Your soul speaks to you through desire. When you desire to learn or do something, pay attention to it. Your inner wisdom is speaking to you.

Schooling trains you to mute this desire and inner wisdom. It is time to honor and cultivate it. At first, it may seem like a quiet whisper that is a stranger to you. As you cultivate deep listening, you will learn to trust your inner calling. Remember: if you are lost, confused, or uncertain, then quit your mind and listen. When you are listening, you aren't thinking. Thinking and analyzing is not the path to clarity.

Planet Earth is most definitely not the center of your personal life. It's merely a background which floats in and out of conscious thought. The truth is that both psychologically and spiritually you are the center of the solar system and the universe. Don't be modest or try to hide the fact. The minute you deny what I just said, you're in full flight from the responsibility this personal centrality entails: to make things better for the rest of us who are on the periphery of your consciousness. - John Taylor Gatto

Your Mind is a Receiver of Wisdom

If you think back to when your child was a baby, you remember a natural wisdom and peace that they had. When my daughter Sage was two days old, I slowly put her into a bassinet beside my bed that a friend had loaned me. She told me it was important not to sleep with your baby and to keep the relationship with your husband primary. As I gently laid Sage down in the bassinet, her eyes flew open and she looked deep into my soul. I saw depths of wisdom and love that I didn't expect. At that moment, I knew that she was a soul sent here to guide and teach me.

It is assumed that losing touch with our innate wellbeing and learning to use our thinking against ourselves is just a normal part of the human experience. *What if this isn't normal? What if it is a result of a schooling system that was designed from fear?*

It might be tricky to see how schooling conditions humans to use their thinking against themselves. It is generally assumed that school is a positive and necessary institution. Any pathology that emerges is attributed to an individual misunderstanding the three psycho-spiritual principles. I see that young people are inherently resilient and creative and are doing their best to survive an institution that systematically denies their consciousness and impedes their creativity, imagination, and innate wisdom.

You were designed to learn. Learning is a natural process for you. You have mirror neurons in your brain that allows you to watch people and then learn to walk, talk, and become a self-sufficient agent designing your life from the inside-out. Learning to talk is the most difficult cognitive process you will master, and you do this without anyone teaching you. You also have an innate intelligence that supplies you with common sense, insights, ah-ha moments, and premonitions.

As we will explore, each individual is unique biologically, neurologically, and spiritually. And every human has an inner voice guiding them to be who they came here to be. When you look at people who have achieved great success in life, most of them attribute their success to following an inner calling or inner knowing.

Learning is an internal process of getting to know self and your place in the world as you explore your gifts and talents. Learning looks different for each individual. It is an emergent process that is soul-directed, not prescribed or predetermined. Learning happens when a person is able to do something that they weren't able to do before.

Babies learn by watching and imitating older people who are modeling movement and language skills. Most babies learn to sit, crawl, walk and talk without anyone teaching them. Learning to speak is the most difficult cognitive task that humans encounter. And babies without cognitive impairment do it without direct instruction.

Your Mind is Not a Muscle

This is so important! Your brain stores information. Your mind is a receiver for infinite intelligence. Your mind is not a muscle that needs to be exercised. Please pause and consider that. Doesn't schooling treat the mind like a muscle?

Listen to John Holt explain that your mind is not a muscle. You can find it on my website CapriceThorsen.com on the Instead of Schooling page.

Your Mind is Not an Information Processor

You and your children were not designed to endlessly process and regurgitate information. Computers are machines that were designed to process information. You are not a machine.

By filling the brain with random disconnected information, your brain becomes so busy, you have no spaced for wisdom to emerge. The problem is that the men who invented schooling in the mid-1800s believed that humans were machines. They denied the existence of a soul, inner life, or consciousness.

How Learning Happens

When you understand how learning happens, schooling will look absurd. Wisdom is your life force. Human learn by creating.

Free Inquiry of a Playful Mind

When a human is free to inquire into personal interests, amazing learning will happen. This is soul-directed learning. The desire for knowledge comes directly from the soul. You cannot get your child to be interested in something. You can introduce a subject to them and see if they are interested. You can share your interests. One of the most valuable things that you can do is be a person who is curious, playful, and invests time in pursuing your own interests.

Most Learning Happens Informally

We are learning all the time. From the moment we wake up until we close our eyes at night, we are learning. Perhaps we even learn and integrate our learning in our dreams. Most of what we learn happens informally, not in school.

> *"Any Yanomami father knows that you don't have to force young children to learn, you just give them the tools they need and then let them play... Talk to gifted scientists, writers, artists, entrepreneurs. You will find they learned like a Yanomami child learns, through keen observation, experimentation, immersion, freedom, participation, through real play and real work, through the kind of free activity where the distinction between work and play disappears. Talk to a really good auto mechanic, carpenter, farmer, fiddle player, web designer, film editor, songwriter, photographer, chef, and you will find they learned the same way."* - Carol Black[32]

The science of learning is still in its infancy and most studies are focused on how students behave in the unnatural environment of school. What we do know is that to learn something, it helps to be interested in it, see that it is relevant to your life, and feel that you are safe and secure as you engage with the learning process.

It's time to expand our view of learning to include informal learning, self-directed learning, modeling, mentoring, curiosity, nature connection, internships, and apprenticeships. When you have an expanded view of learning, then the fear over when and how a child learns to read, write or multiply diminishes. Why? Because the 3 Rs are a very small part of education. And they are best learned by doing integrated projects of the child's own choosing.

In fact, during the past 10 years, scientists have made extraordinary discoveries about how the brain works and develops. What is clear is that everyone is wired to learn differently.

For example, take an 8-year old learner who is a blossoming reader and writer and is following her natural path of learning as the brain and eyes develop and reading and writing is naturally emerging. As she chooses, on her own and in a group of natural learners, projects which capture her interest and imagination — creating an eco-fashion store, making clothing, reading Basher science books, exploring who invented words, studying horses, and cooking — these explorations will expand her ability to read, write and do arithmetic in the natural course of learning.

Contrast this with a fear-based schooling model where parents are being told that they must get their 3 and 4-year-olds ready for kindergarten... Really? Why does a five-year-old need to learn to read and write? "Because if they don't learn the basics now, they will be left behind." Really? What science proves that? The answer: None!

"Imagination is more important than intelligence." – Albert Einstein

My daughter reminded me of something important when she was trying out public school for 7th grade:

Mom, have you noticed that school is designed so that kids in elementary school are learning what they need to get into middle school? Middle school kids are learning what they need for high school. And high school kids are learning what they need to pass tests and get into college. That doesn't make any sense. It's all telling us that we are just preparing for a future that never quite gets here. That's stupid.

The Science of Individuality

> Whatever crushes individuality is despotism,
> by whatever name it may be called, and
> whether it professes to be enforcing the will of
> God or the injunctions of men.
> – John Stuart Mill

Science proves that our bodies are extremely individualized from the nerve endings in different parts of our bodies to the neurons in our brains and hearts. This is important because the information that we get from the outside world varies for each person.[33]

> "The basic answer to the question "Why are
> you an individual?" is that your body in every
> detail, including your entire nervous system and
> your brain (thinking apparatus) is highly
> distinctive. You are not built like anyone else.
> You owe some of your individuality to the fact
> that you have been influenced uniquely by your
> environment, which is not like anyone else's.
> But from all that may be known about basic
> inborn individuality ... it seems clear that the
> amount of individuality we would possess if we
> were all born with exactly the same detailed
> equipment would be puny, indeed, compared
> with the individuality we actually possess."
> – Roger Williams

You will never be able to individualize education in the school system because it is based on belief systems that discount the ingenuity and uniqueness of individual souls.

> *When you deny your own centrality, you necessarily lose some trust in yourself to move mountains. As your self-trust wanes — and school is there to drill you in distrusting yourself (what else do you think it means to wait for the teacher to tell you what to do?) — you lose some self-respect. Without full self-respect, you can hardly love yourself very much because we can't really love those we don't respect (except, curiously enough, by an act of faith).*
> *- John Taylor Gatto*

I'm writing this book as a mother who has home educated her two daughters for almost 18 years. In that time, I've seen that every human is wired differently to learn. My daughters and I are completely different learners. We have unique gifts and strengths, different interests and learn differently. It was a wonderful gift to take a learning styles assessment when they were 4 and 7 and see that they don't learn the way that I do. It took an immense burden off of me to figure it all out. I could trust them as self-directed learners.

My oldest daughter has no phonemic awareness, the classic test for dyslexia, and reads slowly without the ability to sound out words. Yet she got a 100 in ENG 101 and ENG 102 that she took at our local community college. Her strength is her right-brain learning style which allows her to quickly learn choreography and excel as a pre-professional dancer. My youngest daughter loves to read, and we would walk down the street or through a store with her nose in a book. She loves science, writing, acting, and singing.

And she disliked schooling. She tried public school for 7th grade when we moved to a new state and she wanted instant friends.

There is no Average

Todd Rose, author of The End of Average, found that there is no average human, yet we school people as if there are. He debunks our culture of average and shows that human behavior is fluid, not fixed, so we need to design experiences around individuality. There are also no fixed career paths because your character traits are independent of how you learn. And as we discussed above, there is no average human body or brain.

Once you realize that there is no average, you can relax knowing that there is no standard to compare your child to. Watch Todd Rose's TEDx talk The Myth of Average.

Memorizing vs. Understanding

Ayn Rand, in her essay The Comprachicos, makes a valuable distinction between two ways of learning: memorizing and understanding. Rand explains that memorization is achieved by perception and concrete-bound association. In memorizing, students learn discrete bits of information that are associated with each other but not placed into any meaningful or useful context.

> *"To understand means to focus on the content of a given subject (as against the sensory—visual or auditory—form in which it is communicated), to isolate its essentials, to establish its relationship to the previously known, and to integrate it with the appropriate categories of other subjects. Integration is the essential part of understanding." - Ayn Rand*

Understanding is conceptual learning in which you understand abstract concepts and are able to apply them to different areas of your life. To achieve conceptual understanding, you need time to integrate concepts into your reality and make them meaningful.

My mentor, Brent Cameron understood that direct instruction and rote memorization were a small part of the learning process. Used in the context of a meaningful self-chosen project, instruction and memorization can be powerful tools. And they aren't learning.

Economics professor Bryan Caplan, author of *The Case Against Education*, shows in his book that cognitive gains are minimal in college and that most of the knowledge that comes from schooling is "inert", meaning that it can be applied to test questions that mimic the way the information was taught, but people are unable to apply the knowledge to real world situations.

Schooling, with the primary focus on memorization, fills people with "inert knowledge" and conditions people away from using their faculties of reason and logic to come to their own conclusion. They just parrot back answers that they hope are correct.

You might think that this can be corrected by reforming schooling. Schooling was designed this way for a purpose. School is succeeding in achieving its purpose.

The Power of Imagination

When you ask CEOs how they get their best ideas, they will tell you it is when they are driving to work, taking a shower, or walking the dog. They have great ideas, insights, flashes of wisdom when they aren't thinking. When our minds are at rest, fresh ideas come to us. Creativity emerges when we allow our minds to receive wisdom. Another way of putting this is when we are in the flow.

This is why it is so important to let your kids play without end goals. Let them daydream. They are engaging their imaginations, which is a straight path to their inner wisdom. You create that which doesn't yet exist in the world by using your imagination and then making your ideas real. As I said in the beginning of the chapter, creativity is your life force. Education that impairs creativity and imagination is not true education, it is indoctrination.

Truth vs. Society's Misunderstanding

ACHIEVEMENT

Truth: You cannot achieve your way to happiness or peace of mind.

Society's Misunderstanding: Academic achievement is the game of schooling. Whoever processes the most information wins. Children are told explicitly and implicitly that their value and self-worth is dependent upon their achievement in a narrow band of academic activities. The worth/value of students is measured by grades and obedience. Children who are good with symbols and rote memorization and learn in an auditory-sequential way win the game of schooling.

COMPARISON

Truth: You are a unique expression of the divine. You are unique, but not special. Comparing yourself to anyone will cause suffering.

Society's Misunderstanding: Students are continually compared and sorted by teachers and administrators. Parents compare the achievements of their children in school to other kids. *"My kid is an honor roll student"* bumper stickers are everywhere. Grades, GPA, honor roll, and college scholarships are all used to psychologically manipulate children to perform and achieve.

COMPETITION

Truth: Our ground of being is infinite mind. We are all connected, so there is no need to compete. Do your best and let go of the outcome. You are not in control.

Society's Misunderstanding: Students are conditioned to compete for scarce resources (grades, praise, honor roll, etc.) You are responsible for the outcome.

FEAR

Truth: You feel fear when you experience your own fearful thinking. Fear is good when a fight/flight/freeze response could save your life from imminent danger, otherwise it's just a lie your thinking is producing.

Society's Misunderstanding: Uses fear as a weapon of control. Students are threatened with disciplinary action for breaking the rules: coming to school with an uncharged computer, not wearing the proper uniform, talking in class, not doing homework, not following random rules, going to the bathroom without a hall pass.

SHAME

Truth: You are unbreakable and at your core you are pure love and consciousness.

Society's Misunderstanding: You are bad if you don't do your schoolwork, do poorly on a test, or break the rules.

THE ETERNAL NOW

Truth: There is no past or future. The only thing that exists is the eternal now.

Society's Misunderstanding: Work hard now so that you will get rewards in the future.

THE INNER VOICE

Truth: You will be guided every moment by infinite intelligence that comes to you as a loving, calm, quiet voice.

Society's Misunderstanding: Sit still, be quiet, and listen to the teacher. Ignore your body if it wants to move.

CONSCIOUSNESS

Truth: You are conscious and aware. This consciousness allows you to experience your thought-created reality. Your personal mind is connected to infinite mind.

Society's Misunderstanding: Consciousness is the by-product of an advanced brain. It exists locally within your brain and will disappear when you die.

THOUGHT

Truth: You create your moment-by-moment experience of life through your thinking. Thought is a creative power. When you think better, you do better. You are the thinker, not the thoughts.

Society's Misunderstanding: Thinking is an analytic skill that you need to develop by processing information. Thinking is passive and describes an outside reality. Students are taught to navigate life with their intellect, analyzing situations to make decisions. They end up living in their heads.

FEELINGS

Truth: Feelings are your inner GPS system that tells you if you are thinking productive, helpful thoughts, or negative, destructive thoughts.

Society's Misunderstanding: Doesn't acknowledge the inner life of children (or adults).

The net result of schooling is generations of people who are insecure, fearful, and confused. They feel alone and afraid in a cold, uncaring world. They have lost touch with their inner guidance system and are propelled along the conventional path of achievement and success.

At a time when we need human ingenuity, we continue to march young people through a system built for compliance, not wisdom. Welcome to the joyful world of home education. Let's get started!

> *Spiritually contented people are dangerous for a variety of reasons. They don't make reliable servants because they won't jump at every command. They test what is requested against a code of moral principle. Those who are spiritually secure can't easily be driven to sacrifice family relations. Corporate and financial capitalism are hardly possible on any massive scale once a population finds its spiritual center.*
> *- John Taylor Gatto*

Science offers us a lens through which to examine an extremely complex world. And it is only one lens. The other lens is direct experience. You cannot connect with your true Self through your intellect or by seeking with thinking. You must go deeper and go within. Within is not a physical place, it is the place that existed before form.

Yes, the two are different. Your mind is the source of your intelligence. Your brain is the source of your intellect. Your personal mind is connected to a universal mind that guides you lovingly through life. Your personal intellect is a tool that can be used by your intelligence, but it is only a tool.

My Personal Insights

Sydney Banks said you can only share what you personally understand. Here are my personal insights so far...

★ Mostly everyone is insecure because they think they are only human, not divine. From this root of insecurity, they behave in ways that hurt themselves and others. Most people do not understand that they have the intelligence of the universe at their disposal if they can only quiet the chatter of their personal minds.

★ I am not insecure. Unless I think I am.

★ Who I am has nothing to do with how other people behave. I don't care what other people think about me or how they behave towards me. And I remind myself that I cannot control what other people think.

★ I can be fearlessly myself as long as I come from a place of love and understanding.

★ I don't need to love myself unconditionally because I am already love, it is my essence.

★ Behavior is an indication of where people are with their thinking, not who they truly are.

★ When I am in a low mood, it is due to my negative thinking, usually fear based. Once I notice this, I don't need to analyze my thinking or try and figure out what I am thinking because this will just give life to these negative thoughts. Like a coaching client of mine said, "Oh, it would be giving your negative thoughts credit that they don't deserve.". Exactly.

★ I can trust my inner YES and NO. Yes feels light and expansive. No feels heavy and constricting. I feel it mainly in my chest. You can play with this to discover your own inner yes and no.

★ The past doesn't exist except as a memory in my own thinking. I don't think about or dwell on the past because it steals the only thing that is real – this very moment.

★ I am unbreakable. I am a whole being who has innate health and peace of mind.

★ My new mantra is PYT (pronounced pyd) -- a Danish word that means you accept a situation that is beyond your control and won't invest any energy thinking about it. You won't worry about it or stress over it even if it doesn't match your personal preferences.

You Are What You are Seeking

You are not broken. Let go of everything that has happened in your life. Let go of every idea you have about who you are and what you can do.

Universal Mind, Universal Consciousness, and Universal Thought are all pure, impersonal love. That is the only thing that is real. The rest is made up. Your self-image. Your limitations.

Once we connect with our inner perfection, we stop seeking that which we don't need.

> *"People can never get enough of that which*
> *they don't need." - Dr. Bill Pettit*

When we realize that we ARE love, we stop looking for love outside of ourselves. We can go into the world and form relationships with people without needing anything from them. We don't need love, approval, or anything else. You are love. You are limitless. To go home, head towards feelings of love and understanding.

We are one. Unless we are conditioned to believe that we are small, physical beings carrying around brains. This is how we are conditioned by schooling and innocent parents. It creates a schooled mindset.

What is human spirit? It is the part of us that is connected to divine universal intelligence. It is pure love. Not romantic love. Unconditional love. It shines through in a crisis. It burst through after 9/11.

Forced government schooling has left us with a casual disregard for life because it trains us to view the world and ourselves as machines. It was designed this way because the men who invented school were religious humanists who did not believe that there was a universal intelligence. The U.S. Supreme Court ruled in 2014 that Humanism is a religion.

Compulsory schooling is producing people who feel broken and unworthy because it denies the existence of our soul. Schooling writes our story for us and then deposits us into it.

We are never guided to understand how our human and spiritual operating systems work. Instead we are taught to value our intellect over our intelligence. Our intellect is merely a computer-like tool that our egos use to make sense of the world. We cannot get anything out of our brains except the information that we put into it.

We are forced to strive and compete in a quest to feel secure and worthy of love. The damage schooling has done includes environmental devastation as this schooled populace tries to consume its way to feeling whole, okay, and loved.

We invest 18+ years and $1.3 trillion dollars per year breaking children's spirits to make them compliant so that they can be controlled. Then the self-help and personal development industries make $60 billion dollars trying to heal their adult spirits.

This is an invitation to evolve our understanding of learning and to awaken to our spiritual operating system. When we embrace the spiritual dimension of life, we will heal ourselves and planet earth.

The Power of the Individual

> *Everyone holds his fortune in his own hands,*
> *like a sculptor the raw material he will fashion*
> *into a figure. But it's the same with that type of*
> *artistic activity as with all others: We are merely*
> *born with the capability to do it. The skill to*
> *mold the material into what we want must be*
> *learned and attentively cultivated.*
> *— Johann Wolfgang Von Goethe*

You didn't come with operating instructions or a manual. You came with something better -- divine intelligence that will guide you every step of the way, moment by moment. Unless you succumb to your fear-based ego thought system.Unfortunately, because school was invented by men who did not believe that there is a divine or universal intelligence powering all life, schooling disavows this power and trains you to rely on your ego thought system.

The United States was founded on the principle of political equality and the understanding that there are natural laws of individual rights. Why was there such a belief in the power of the individual? Because it is the individual who has imagination, creativity, and reason. Society cannot claim any of these powers.

All creativity and inventions come from within an individual.

PART 4: Educating for Creativity, Resilience & Happiness

Getting Started - Make Learning and Creating a Winning Game

If anyone has made you believe that you are not up to the challenge of educating your own children without school, I am here to tell you that you are. You were your child's first teacher and you know your child better than anyone other than that child. In partnership with your child, you can do this. You are both wired to learn and when you open your mind to the small inner voice of wisdom, you will know what to do in any moment. And you will operate from a place of love. What a gift to your child!

I learned from one of my coaches that we are all playing a game of life. It is up to us to choose how we design that game. Now, I know that your child's education is important. And if we set up this game correctly, you will see that there is no way that you or your child can lose. Unfortunately, many parents simply try to reproduce school at home and that is a tough game to win. So, let's get started.

The Natural Phases of Deschooling

Reproducing School at Home

Most parents who have moved from conventional schooling to homeschooling, try to reproduce all of the academics from school. Often, they will buy expensive, pre-packaged all-in-one curriculum or they will sign up for an expensive online school. From my direct experience and that of coaching other parents, the majority of homeschool curriculum is focused on information processing and memorization just like schooling and so is just as boring. I'll put my favorite home education resources in the Resource chapter so that you can pick and choose based on your child's interests and learning style.

Entering the Battle Zone

It is impossible to reproduce school at home because you don't have the methods of fear and shame that outside authorities wield. The sooner you give up this losing battle the better.

Giving Up

Many parents will swing to the other extreme after heated battles and bruised relationships. They just let their kids do whatever they want without any boundaries or restrictions. Often this looks like playing video games all day or being on electronics. Then the parents have moments of extreme self-doubt and insecurity and will swing back to school at home. This pendulum may swing many times until they relax into an eclectic, self-directed approach.

Beginning Anew: The Quilt Method

I love the book, *Composing a Life*, by Mary Catherine Bateson. She uses the analogy of a quilt as your life. You are always working on one square but, often until you get to the end, and see the beautiful quilt you have created, you're not sure where all of the pieces fit. And so it is with home educating. If you look at it as a messy, non-linear process of many fits and starts, a process of creative invention, then you will not be bothered with the box of unfinished projects sitting in your garage. You will not be plagued by the tyranny of the paper trail that you might think you need to prove that learning is happening. Allow your child to self-direct their learning, set boundaries on technology to set your mind at ease, and enjoy the natural learning process.

Step 1: Design Principles

Borrowing a page from design thinking, as you set out on your journey to design an educational environment and path for your children, it's helpful to have some design principles. These are some that I recommend you consider:

Love: Always make decisions and take actions from a place of love. If you are feeling frustrated, angry, overwhelmed, or anxious, then take a moment and let your thinking settle down before you talk to your child or make a decision. Take a walk, stretch, listen to music, just pause and let your mind settle and your natural state of peace return.

Preserving Wholeness: Your child has everything inside to grow into an amazing adult. Like the acorn will grow into an oak tree, your child has the wisdom, resources, intelligence, and gifts to follow the soul's calling. Your work is to provide the best environment and curate resources to optimize the growth. You are like the gardener who is making sure the soil is rich, there is enough sun and rain. But you don't need to modify the seed. It is perfect.

Play: Humans learn so much from play. Play may look a lot different than when you were a child. Who is to say that playing the latest video game with friends is any less stimulating than playing chess?

Curiosity & Imagination: Curiosity drives children to explore the world and figure out their place in it. My daughter coined a term when she was 4 years old: curiation which combines curiosity and imagination. Let your children play uninterrupted when they are younger and ask your children what they are curious about and what they are interested in learning and investing their time doing. Their answers might surprise you.

Non-Judgement: You are the space of impersonal awareness. This space does not judge. When your personal thinking starts judging your family's educational path or your child's choices as good or bad you will start feeling less free and stressed. It's okay. It is part of the journey. I think every home educating parent I have met has had moments of self-doubt. As your child transitions from one developmental stage to the next, oftentimes old interests are cast aside and new ones don't immediately appear. There might be moments of boredom and frustration. This is a great time to reach out to experienced home educators for reassurance and guidance. Trust the learning process. Trust your children.

Fostering Self-Agency: It is easy for adults to jump in and figure something out for younger people or try and solve situations. The more you can let your children find their own solutions and overcome their challenges, knowing that you've got their back, they will gain confidence in their own abilities and develop self-agency.

Creativity: We are born to create. Life is creative. We are part of life. Just look around you at the multitude of birds, plants, and animals. I believe that people are most happy and satisfied when they are creating in the way that they most enjoy. If you can view creating as your curriculum, you will never have a boring day.

Step 2: Your Relationship to Your Child Is Most Important

I learned from Brent Cameron that families are the smallest learning unit, not the individual. Children learn constantly from what their parents and siblings do. We learn in relationships with other people. We have a strong need to belong to a community. The human brain is wired for relationships! The human brain loves to learn. But if the conditions for these neurobiological states are not attended to, we all experience the negative effects of a compromised nervous system which correlates with everything we do and are. – Lori Desautels

> If we feel safe and loved, our brain specializes in cooperation, play, and exploration! If we are constantly feeling unloved, frightened or unwanted, the brain specializes in managing feelings of fear and abandonment. – Bessel Van Der Volk

Lori Desautels, PhD, author of *Unwritten, The Story of a Living System* tells us that students who go to school from kindergarten through 12th grade typically spend more than 13,000 hours of their developing brain's time in the presence of teachers. She coaches teachers to post the following four questions in their classroom:

A. Am I important to someone here?
B. Am I good at something here?
C. Am I able to affect change of my world here?
D. Can I share my gifts with someone here?

It is important for your child to know that they matter, they have natural gifts and talents, they don't have to be good at everything, they can change the world and their work is to share their gifts with the world.

Step 3: Shifting from a Schooled to an Ecological Mindset

I was first introduced to the concept of ecology in education when I began working with the co-founder of the SelfDesign Learning Foundation, Brent Cameron. Brent was a student of Gregory Bateson's work and often referenced Bateson's statement: "The major problems in the world are the result of the difference between how nature works and the way people think." Brent had an expansive view of learning that was not limited to rote memorization or instruction. He initially called it "natural learning" and often said that humans are designed to learn.

What we see in the world today is a battle between collectivism and individualism. Schooling is a toxic mix of collectivism and individualism where students compete with each other by doing the same set of mundane tasks.

The collectivist mindset emerged in the early 1800s out of fear and anger at the increasing inequities in the global economy. This mindset is taught in the unnatural learning environment of schooling. The economy is viewed as a fixed pie that needs to be distributed equally among all people. What collectivists fail to understand is that when an individual creates something, the pie expands. When an entrepreneur invents something or builds a company, the economy expands and there is more opportunity for everyone.

The individualistic mindset lends itself to distortion by narcissism as the world and economy is viewed as a zero-sum game. The individual wins only when others lose.

We need to transcend these mindsets and embrace an ecological mindset. An ecological mindset allows for the individual and the group Planet Earth to flourish. It could be viewed as collectivist independence, where every member of the group maintains their individual uniqueness and applies their gifts and talents to a shared purpose of the group.[34]

Schooled Mindset: Belief that you are a separate mechanical being with a body that carries around a mechanical brain. Belief that the world is a cold, uncaring, mechanistic machine and that we are all separate. To survive, you need to strive and compete for scarce resources. You are in control. There is no higher power operating in the world.

Ecological Mindset: An ecological mindset acknowledges that our experience of life comes from our thinking. We are 7.5 billion souls with overlapping experiences of life. We are all animated by the same source of life. We are all connected to a universal mind that is the source of our insights, creativity, and imagination. We are spiritual beings having a human experience. Our essence is well-being, peace of mind, and joy that gets covered up by negative, fear-based thinking that has been conditioned into us.

The Ecological Mindset incorporates what we know from quantum physics and consciousness research. When you adopt this worldview, you stop breaking spirits. Your natural state is an ecological mindset. The schooled mindset has been conditioned into you, and you can let it go right now.

Schooled Mindset	Ecological Mindset
Student as Object	Learner as Co-Creator
Fear-based	Love-based
Outside-In Living	Inside-Out Living
Heavy Ecological Footprint	Light Ecological Footprint
Burnt Out	Resilient
Anxious	Peaceful
Depressed	Joyful
Compare and Compete	Look Inside
Special-Better	Unique-Equal
Consumer	Creator
Follower	Leader
Competitive	Cooperative
Striving	Flowing
Unconscious	Conscious
Reactive	Intentional
Low empathy for others	We're all in this together
Future focused	Present

Step 4: The Art of Self Direction

Giving our children control of their own education is certainly a risky business. All guarantees that they are keeping pace with their peers are abandoned and replaced with a simple trust that they will explore life of their own initiative. - Brent Cameron

The focus of my work in education both at home and creating alternative learning experiences has been around self-direction. I created an entire online course on Self Directed Learning for the California Teachers College, so I will do my best to make this section short and sweet.

One of the biggest misunderstandings about self-directed learning is that it means a child is learning alone. Nope. A child is choosing how to invest her time and often it will involve group classes, working with mentors, and sometimes doing conventional academics that looks very much like school.

How does one become self directed? People are naturally self directed especially when they are engaged in activities that they enjoy. Sage has been super self directed over the years as she has taught herself to do complicated hairstyles, makeup, and crafting by watching YouTube videos. I could never teach her these, because I have no personal interest and also no innate talent for it.

She is less self directed when it comes to something that she believes she should do but doesn't really want to do, for example math. So, the question then becomes, "why do you want to learn math and how can we make that happen?" Her answer was that she wanted to do the math classes necessary to get into a good college. So, she did algebra 1, geometry, and algebra 2 and next year will be doing an online college calculus class to get it out of the way. I talk frequently about how useless algebra 2 is for most people and since it was important to Sage to check off the box, it was a meaningful experience for her. And I'm happy to say that our relationship survived me tutoring her through the class.

Sage told me when she was 9 years old that she wanted someone to design her learning projects for her and then give her the freedom to complete the projects the way that she wanted to. She liked hands-on learning, games, and puzzles, and I found lots of fun things for her to do. It was a process of trial and error, strewing interesting things around the house, and being willing to abandon a project when it wasn't going well.

When she turned 13, she wanted more academics. We chose Acellus Academy because it is video based and offers instant feedback in the form of quizzes and tests. It looks very much like school online and it worked for Sage. She also took courses at the local community college to get early college credits. A significant portion of her time is invested at her dance studio and now at her part-time job.

My youngest daughter invests her time reading, writing, singing, acting, playing with friends, and cooking. She really doesn't like math, so we do it together to make sure she has basic numeracy to get along in life. She enjoys learning through books and workbooks, and hates doing video lessons. When she was 7 years old, I got her the Basher Science series of books and she learned about the human body, planet earth, and chemistry in a way that was interesting and engaging for her. At 12 years old, I would take her to the local bookstore, and she would choose Shakespeare and mystery novels. She loves to write and won a Daughters of the American Revolution essay contest. But when she was in public school for 7th grade, she started hating writing, reading, and music - all of her former and now recovered passions.

Step 5: Understand the Different Ages and Stages

There is no timetable for learning. You don't want to glue wings to a caterpillar, as Brent Cameron pointed out in his critique of schooling. Do not view babies and young children as immature, defective adults. Recent studies have found that, in some ways, young children are smarter than adults.

Babies

Babies know more than we think they do. This doesn't mean that they need artificial activities or make work. Children under the age of five are not good at making plans or focusing on goals. They are busy getting to know their environment and are in awe and wonder about everything. Let them stay enchanted with the natural world. The young brain has many more neurons than adult brains[35]. It is plastic and flexible. Just allow babies to play and create a safe environment for open exploration.

Ages 2-7: Let them Play

Young children learn through play. They learn to cooperate, negotiate, and solve conflicts. Children learn how the world works. They watch adults and then pretend to do what they do. Pre-schoolers have been observed using probability and imagination to predict outcomes. Children under the age of 5 tend to learn a foreign language more quickly than older children and adults. Psychologist Peter Gray, author of Free to Learn, is an expert in learning through play. I highly recommend you check out his excellent articles on his Psychology Today blog.

Ages 8-12: Projects Rule

The Wondertree Center was divided into broad age brackets: Age 5, 6-8, 9-12, and 13+. These groupings were based on Brent's experience with the changing interests and abilities of learners. In Finland, schools begin formal math instruction with children at the age of 8. Brent also found that around that age, many children are eager for more conceptual learning. This is no hard and fast rule. As we saw in the Science of Individuality and There is No Average, each child comes with their own propensity and wiring for learning.

I did see an intellectual blossoming and emotional maturation around the age of 8 and 9. These are the early bridge years between being young children who love free play and exploration and children who want to learn more about the world and their place in it. We did lots of science experiments, geocaching, and I started a self-directed learning center for ages 8-13. We brought in an art teacher and partnered with a nature teacher to take the kids on excursions one afternoon a week. Projects varied by the week and were inspired by the interests of the kids and the mentors. The kids love doing walkabouts in the community and exploring their place in it.

When given a choice of how to invest their time, these learners wanted to be active, outside, and part of the community. I highly recommend at this age to find places where they can contribute their gifts and feel like valuable members of the community, whether it is volunteering on a local farm, animal shelter, or other business.

Ages 13+: Give them Freedom and Have Lots of Conversations

Around the age of 12 or 13, many kids want to do more focused work. This is when, if they have had enough time to play, discover, and just be, they tend to want to do more deep learning and some more academic pursuits.

My oldest daughter decided she wanted to make sure she was at grade level in all of her high school work. Checking off the boxes was important to her. That might not look like self-direction to some people, and all of her academic choices were self-chosen. She liked some classes (history) better than others (math, chemistry). It was important that she stayed true to herself and followed her inner knowing. She will be graduating high school with 10 college credits.

I have discovered how important it is for me to be there as a loving, non-judgmental guide to help them transition into adulthood. No conversation is off limits. I've heard about all of the shenanigans of other teenagers. I'm not a perfect mother; there is no perfect parent. By allowing my daughters to self-direct their learning, they have learned to self-direct their lives. They don't engage in any self-destructive behavior because they have nothing to rebel against. And we moved through and healed from an extremely traumatic divorce when I found out their father was seeing other women. He made choices that didn't include our daughters' well-being. It was a rough patch and love and openness got us through to a place where we are all thriving.

I learned that it's not my job to protect my kids from life. Life is a full-contact sport. My work is to help them gracefully navigate it, connected to the inner wisdom and using their emotions as their GPS.

Step 6: What is Worth Learning?

The best way to approach learning design and curriculum is to realize that most textbooks and curricula are inherently boring, fact-based, and often inaccurate. Free yourself from the tyranny of textbooks. The textbook industry is big business and one of the main reasons that there is no innovation in school. That said, there are lots of new and engaging learning resources that you can use with your children. I have put links to resources I like on my website CapriceThorsen.com.

My own experience, as well as that of other researchers, suggests that rather than creating enthusiasm and stimulating thinking, textbooks usually deaden the minds of students and alienate them from learning. - Mordechai Gordon

There Are No Basics

There is so much information currently in the world, you can't even hope to learn 1%. There are no basics. The Common Core was invented by people with no education background. They were bureaucrats and politicians, not teachers. If you let go of the mistaken notion that there is a fixed set of information your kid needs to become an adult, then life gets a whole lot simpler and more fun.

I remember when Kayli was 5 years old, she became fascinated with animals. If anyone in the family had any questions about animals, she was our go-to person. She was equipped with lots of books on animals and an iPad. She became fascinated with sharks, so we binge watched shark week. She became entranced with science, so we got the Basher science series and she told me all about the b-cells and t-cells that heal our bodies. This is how learning happens. In the free inquiry of a relaxed, playful mind.

Contrast that with Kayli's experience of public school 7 years later. She started hating her favorite pastimes - reading, writing, and music. She sat there day after day as they tried to stuff her full of information that she was neither interested in nor cared about. As the end of school approached and the state standardized test loomed ever closer, the pace of this information stuffing became frenetic. The teachers got increasingly stressed. It was a mess. All for a test that somebody made up. It is absurd to think that all 12-year olds need to know certain things that most adults probably don't know which will be forgotten by next year.

The Smorgasbord Approach

Okay, I'm 25% Danish and love smorgasbords where you can choose a little bit of lots of different foods to eat. This is a great way to introduce the world to your child.

Your child will tell you when they are ready for or interested in something. View yourself as the guide along the side and the curator of cool resources. If your child is interested in something, then make sure he has the resources, mentors, and support to pursue that interest. A wonderful way to introduce new things is to strew books and fun resources around the house for your child to discover. Another way is to be actively engaged in creative projects that you love to model creating as learning.

When Sage wanted to learn to play the guitar, I found an inexpensive electric guitar and we tried several guitar teachers until she found one that she clicked with. Sometimes you need to try many mentors until you find the right one for your kid. Also, many adults act differently when they are with adults than when they are one-on-one with children. Teach your kids to trust their intuition about people.

Teaching Reading

Once again, don't think that you need to reproduce schooling when it comes to teaching reading. The majority of kids learn to read when they are interested and ready. The majority of kids learn to read when they are interested and ready. A friend of mine who specialized in teaching Gifted students told me that gifted kids either learn to read early (before the age of 5) or late (after the age of 12). The range of ages when a child learns to read is quite wide. It is simply not true that every child should be reading at age 5.

I worked with a Special Education teacher at SelfDesign, who was also a reading specialist. She told me that 30% of kids need help learning to read. Here is a quick test to see if your child is struggling with reading and needs help. If you child wants to read and asks for help, then get help. If they are not interested in reading, then make sure you have an environment at home that treasures reading. Read a lot by yourself and to your child. If you do decide to teach reading, don't use whole word instruction. I'll explain more later.

My youngest loves to read and always had her nose in a book since she was 7 years old. She read the Harry Potter series 3 times before she was 9. And she started to hate reading in public school. Have you ever had to read something and annotate it? That is almost a sure-fire way to kill the love of reading. Here's my recommendation: read around your kids if you love to read. Have a house that supports literacy. Read to them a lot when they are young. Allow them to read what they want to read.

Dyslexia

My oldest daughter is dyslexic. She has no phonemic awareness, which means that she cannot sound out words. Home educating your child is one of the best things you can do if your child is dyslexic. The current Diagnostic and Statistical Manual of Mental Disorders (DSM–5) took out dyslexia as a diagnosis, so if you do take your child to be assessed, the psychologist will give a diagnosis of a specific learning disability in reading and writing. I think that viewing dyslexia as a disability is disempowering. Sir Richard

Branson, himself dyslexic agrees. He says, "Dyslexic minds have exactly the skills we need for the workforce of tomorrow". He attributes his success in business to his dyslexia. He was a poor student in school and wildly successful in life. He has funded the creation of MadeByDyslexia.com

Watch the videos on MadeByDyslexia.com

When my daughter was 5 years old, she asked me for reading glasses because she said her eyes weren't working. She really wanted to read. A normal eye exam showed she was slightly far-sighted which was normal for her age. I then took her to two developmental ophthalmologists who recommended extensive and expensive eye exercises in their office. We tried them. She hated them. They gave her intense headaches. There is conflicting research on whether or not developmental eye exercises help or not.

We did not figure out that she was dyslexic until she was 13 despite her getting an IEP when she was 7 from our local school district's psychologist. The remediation they recommended at that time did not work.

If your child asks for support, like mine did, get your child tested to see if they have phonemic awareness. We consulted lots of reading and dyslexia specialists. I'm not sure why nobody tested her until she was 13 for phonemic awareness, the classic definition of dyslexia.

Many people recommend Orton-Gillingham. It didn't work for us because it is task-oriented, sequential, and boring. Sage is a right-brain visual learner who learns by seeing the big picture first and then fitting the pieces in. Pretty much the opposite of all Orton-Gillingham approaches. Sage did work with a woman who was getting her PhD in Special Education with a focus on reading for 1.5 years. They painstakingly went through all of the phonemes so that Sage could memorize and pronounce them. It helped a little bit. It wasn't the magic bullet.

What we've done is helped Sage focus on her strengths. Manipulation of language and symbols isn't her strength. Sage reads slowly but competently and prefers video courses over textbooks or lectures.

If your child struggles with reading, do some research on famous and successful people with dyslexia who succeed because they have other strengths. Many wildly successful people including Paul Orfalea, Sir Richard Branson, Thomas Edison, Henry Ford, Ted Turner and even Albert Einstein have/had dyslexia. Every child is unique, and there is no one approach that works for everyone. Just remember, as you try different approaches: your child is not broken.

Schools Teach Illiteracy

Most children in public schools who are classified with learning disabilities have reading disabilities.[36] There is a lot of conflicting research on this, but one thing is for certain: whole word instruction produces what looks like dyslexia.

- Only 13.5% of 15-year olds in the U.S. can distinguish between fact and opinion on the PISA reading exam.[37]

- More than 75% of students at two-year colleges and more than 50% of students at four-year colleges score below the proficient level of literacy. They cannot perform complex literacy tasks, such as comparing credit card offers with different interest rates or summarizing the arguments of newspaper editorials.

- 52% of American adults function at the basic or below-basic reading level, meaning that they cannot find places on a map, calculate the cost of office supplies from a catalog or compare viewpoints in two editorials.[38]

Many education reformers and critics claim that whole word instruction was purposefully introduced into schools in the early 1900s to reduce literacy. Whether this is true or not, there have been numerous studies and excellent books that show, without a doubt, that the way in which reading is taught in public schools creates the crisis of illiteracy that we see today.

Patrick Groff, Ed.D tells us that educational malpractice is the root cause of most cases of dyslexia and illiteracy. The Follow Through project in the 1960s and 1970s found that Direct Instruction, which includes Phonics instruction, is the most effective way to teach reading to struggling readers. Yet public schools and teacher training programs across the country continue to use Whole Word instruction.

Louisa Cook Moats found that:

> *Unfortunately, state certification practices, pre-service teacher training, and the social contexts of schools do not adequately prepare reading and writing teachers for the demands of classroom practice. More specifically, neither undergraduate nor graduate training of teachers typically requires the command of language structure necessary to teach reading and spelling well. Consequently, teachers are inadequately prepared to teach emergent literacy, reading, and spelling to beginning readers and those encountering reading failure.*[39]

Since the 1960s we have known that the way teachers are being trained to teach reading is ineffective and yet not much has changed. Don't you wonder why?

Writing

Some kids love to write, others hate it, many are neutral. My youngest daughter loves to write but this love of writing was almost wiped out in her year of public school because of their focus on the mechanics of writing and vocabulary rather than the creativity of writing and the importance of communication.

Sage took ENG 101 and 102 at our local community college as a high school junior last year. She got a 100 in both classes. Her instructor was more focused on a student's ability to communicate and think. She does both well. She writes like she speaks in a very conversational and easy to read way.

As with reading, the focus is on communicating ideas. Today, the ability to do videos and podcasts is just as valid a skill as writing. There are fabulous writing programs including Brave Writer and Cover Story that make writing fun and relevant.

Maths

Many adults cannot do elementary level math. An informal Buzzfeed quiz[40] found that their staff got a 50% on basic math questions. These are successful, employed adults so it begs the question of the usefulness of most school math.

Math is the subject that homeschooling families struggle with the most. This is mainly because school math is not real math. And the math you will find on standardized tests is also different from school math.

If your child is heading to college, it helps to know that Algebra is the most frequently failed course in high school and community college. There is a movement afoot to get rid of Algebra as a requirement. While algebra is foundational for advanced, conceptual math, statistics and data science are often more useful for many professions.

To start this conversation, I invite you to read A Mathematician's Lament by Paul Lockhart. It is a wonderful essay on how school math destroys the love of mathematics and doesn't help children appreciate the beauty of math.

One of my favorite math resources is Stanford Professor, Jo Boaler's, YouCubed website. Dr. Boaler specializes in teaching math teachers how to teach math. I took the beta version of her parent course when it first came out and it was transformational in helping me to reframe math. Here are some things that I learned:

- Embrace mistakes: Making a mistake on a math problem is the best way to grow your brain.
- Timed math tests are one of the worst things on the planet.
- Math is best learned cooperatively so that children can see there are many different ways to solve the same problem.

On her YouCubed website, there is a course for students and lots of fun math tasks.

Neither of my children were doing grade-level math throughout elementary school or middle school because it wasn't enjoyable for them and it wasn't an interest. And when it came time to do Algebra 1, Geometry, and Algebra 2, my daughter did just fine and got A's in all of her online courses. What school doesn't tell you is that an Algebra 1 class will go over all of the skills a child needs for that course. And by the time you get to these higher-level courses, they are allowed to use a calculator. As long as your child understands the concept of multiplication and division, they will not need to do procedures like long division. Think about it… how often do you do long division? I usually just open my smartphone and use the calculator.

We did math games and songs when they were younger. We cooked together and played with fractions. My daughter is doing an online college Calculus class her Senior year of high school to get it out of the way and because you only pay for it if you pass. I figure they've put a lot of time and effort into producing a quality class that young people will pass. I will put my favorite resources in the appendix for you.

For your design process, think about the math that you use on a daily basis. Fractions are helpful for cooking. Counting money is necessary for shopping. Measuring is needed for sewing and building. Trigonometry is useful if you are making furniture. Data science is necessary so that you can analyze news reports and see if data is being manipulated to support someone's opinion. Dividing fractions? Geometric proofs?

One of my favorite math resources is Constructing the Universe by Michael S. Schneider. He wrote a book by the same name and activity books that take you through each number one through nine to appreciate math in the context of nature, art, and architecture.

Science

My daughters loved science and exploring the natural world until they got a taste of school science. School science is trapped by the materialist, reductionist paradigm. It teaches the parts of a plant but not the magnificence of plants. It fails to teach that plants are the most efficient creations and can communicate between each other. I highly recommend that you just let your kids explore and stay in awe and wonder about the world around them. My youngest daughter was entranced by the Basher science books and spent most of her time in nature.

When you are looking for a science curriculum to satisfy college entrance requirement, choose one that is based on conceptual science and not highly mathematical. Lots of hands-on experiments makes science real.

Economics

You cannot function well as an adult without an understanding of money, finances, and economics. Trust me on this one. I did get an MBA in finance from Carnegie Mellon University and received a scholarship my second year there for best female student in finance. My economics classes at Carnegie Mellon were calculus based. I even dreamed Calculus my first few months there. Pretty scary!

This was one of my only non-negotiables for my daughters. I wasn't going to let them enter adulthood without a solid foundation in economics. There are two primary schools of economics: Keynesian and Austrian. Public schools and most colleges teach Keynesian economics and advocate for government manipulation of the economy. Austrian economics advocate for free markets and minimal government action. I was grateful to have taken a course at Carnegie Mellon taught by Herbert Simon who won a Nobel Prize for Economics. I will never forget Dr. Simon telling my class, "the only function of government is to reallocate income". That has always stuck with me.

My personal understanding of economics is that innovation and entrepreneurship happen at the individual level. Governments and bureaucracies are not innovative. They do not create jobs. They create nothing. There is a role for government, but it is not creating or growing businesses. Federal and state governments collect taxes and then divvy up the money. Bureaucrats take the pie and cut it into slices. Entrepreneurs build businesses. When a person creates a business, jobs are created. The whole pie grows bigger. Few entrepreneurs are greedy capitalists. Most start their business because they have a great idea and a burning passion to make it real. There are easier ways to make money than starting a business.

Some of my favorite economics resources are offered for free at the Foundation for Economic Education website (fee.org). I, *Pencil*, *Economics in One Lesson*, and *The Law* are classic book and a great place to start. I also like *Whatever Happened to Penny Candy* and the Uncle Eric series.

It's also important to understand how our monetary system works (or doesn't work). Most people don't understand that our whole monetary system is based on debt. Money is created when an individual, company, organization, or government institution takes out a loan. When you investigate the history of money, your view of the whole system changes. I include some of these resources on my website at CapriceThorsen.com.

Step 7: Learning Goals –
A Flexible Living Plan

SelfDesign uses mind maps to help learners access their creative right brain to design a learning plan for the year. The intention is to tap into a learner's inner knowing and transcend their "shoulds" and intellect. Tony Buzan was the inventor of Mind Maps and his organization offers a free introductory course on mind mapping.

I saw that this works well for some kids and other kids aren't so excited by the prospect. I found lying on the floor with my children and a big sheet of paper, colored markers, and intensely curious and playful minds helped to start the conversation.

In August and September, there is a natural rhythm of renewal and excitement. Ask your child questions like spark great conversations:

"How do you want to invest your time?"
"What questions do you have about the world?"
"What do you enjoy doing?"

Be in a space of loving, impersonal non-judgement – which is who you really are. When you don't judge playing chess as more important and valid than playing video games, then your child will feel free to be exactly who they are in this moment. When you can let go of the unnatural timetable that schooling has imposed on learning, you rest easy in knowing that your child cannot fall behind because learning is not a race.

The important part of this process is putting your child in the middle and designing learning experiences around the child. Start with a beginner's mind. Admit that you don't know what will appear.

Don't try to force your kid into a pre-packaged curriculum. It looks like it is the easy answer at first. But I have yet to meet a child for which this approach really works.

Step 8: Government & Economics Education

George Washington said, "A primary object... should be the education of our youth in the science of government. In a republic, what species of knowledge can be equally important? And what duty more pressing... than communicating it to those who are to be the future guardians of the liberties of the country?"

You cannot participate intelligently in a democracy if you don't understand how it works and if you cannot tell fact from fiction when you are reading or watching the news. Most schooled people can do neither.

- 43% of Americans don't know there are 3 branches of government in the U.S.[41]

- 66% of Americans don't know where "We hold these truths to be self-evident, that all men are created equal."

- 53% of Americans don't know what the first 10 amendments to the U.S. Constitution are called.

The NEA purposefully replaced the study of the constitution and the science of government with the study of local "social agencies". This is the reason that most people are ignorant of how the government works and cannot even tell you what one of the Bill of Rights are. You cannot demand protection for your rights if you don't know what they are.

From the National Education Association's Commission on the Reorganization of Secondary Education, we get the Cardinal principles of secondary education[42], which changed the study of history and govenmrent to "social studies":

*"While all subjects should contribute to good citizenship, the social studies - geography, history, civics, and economics - should have this as their dominant aim. Too frequently, however, **does mere information, conventional in value and remote in bearing, make up the content of social studies. History should so treat the growth of institutions that their present value may be appreciated.** Geography should show the interdependence of men while it shows their common dependence on nature. **Civics should concern itself less with constitutional questions and remote government functions, and should direct attention to social agencies close at hand** and to the informal activities of daily life that regard and seek the common good."*

A 2016 survey from the American Council of Trustees and Alumni (ACTA) found that, "When asked to identify the rights guaranteed by the First Amendment, one-third of Americans could not name a single right; 43% could not even name freedom of speech as one of those rights." [43]The ACTA report A Crisis in Civic Education states that, "The problem starts in public high schools that are placing less emphasis on civics education than in the past, and results from the National Assessment of Educational Progress show it's having an impact."

In 2010, NEAP test results showed that while nearly all high school seniors studied civics, less than a quarter scored proficient or above. A staggering 36 percent did not have even a basic understanding and couldn't "describe forms of political participation available in a democracy" or "provide simple interpretations of nontext-based information such as maps, charts, tables, graphs, and cartoons," according to the report. That was

> *before NEAP officials cut the civics portion*
> *from the test in 2014 citing budget issues.[44]*

The information that children are fed in school is highly biased towards a utopian future where the mass of people is controlled by a ruling elite with a specific worldview.

John Taylor Gatto shows us that between 1890 and 1920, the children's literature industry because "a creator not a reflector" of values as issues like death, evil, and the future were systematically removed from children's books and replaced by the "individual child free from the web of family and community".

Francis Fitzgerald, author of America Revised, invested her time reading the textbooks that are used in school and says this,

> *"The purpose of history teaching in the schools has been essentially to manipulate children's behavior, rather than to teach them how to learn. I began to wonder how that ever crept into these books. And I found out through looking at educational documents and interviewing teachers and so on that this has really been true since the beginning of the century. And if you look at the, sort of, important decisions that were made in the National Education Association at the time, that it's set down there that the only history that should be taught is one that will produce certain kinds of social action, you know. Its history taught not from the present backwards, but as it were, from the future backwards. From the kind of future that's already determined by the wishes of the teachers.*
>
> *But they do a terrible job of it...Because what they're doing is not teaching history, but giving kids instructions in patriotism, in good citizenship, and this and that. Well, supposing*

they could actually make everyone into perfect citizens? Well, that would be quite something. But it turns out that they're a terrible failure on, again, an intellectual plane. There have been so many studies that show that kids retain almost nothing of what they learn from this. They're bored to death.

Rest easy if you think that schools are really teaching kids how to think critically. You can do better. There are lots of fantastic free resources for teaching history, government, and economics in an interesting, engaging and useful way that I will include in the resources section.

Step 9: The Importance of Rhythm

It is incredibly important to establish a rhythm for the days and weeks. I love the book, A Child's Seasonal Treasury by Betty Jones. As a seasoned Waldorf educator, she provides lots of songs, rituals, poems, games, and crafts to celebrate the changing of the natural seasons. It works spectacularly with young children.

I created large, color-coded wall calendars to help my daughters navigate the days. We had breakfast and lunch together and they worked on individual projects when I worked, because I have been a working, home educating mom since my daughters were born. And I have been fortunate to be able to work from home.

Regio Emilia views the learning environment as a teacher. Look at your home and see how it works as a learning tool. Do you have a reading nook, art center, science corner?

You will fall into a rhythm as you notice what makes sense. And some days, the rhythm just doesn't seem to work. Everything seems like it happens on the off-beat. We all have those days.

Things that can help you establish rhythm:

- Seasons
- Holidays
- Birthdays
- Morning and Afternoon check-ins
- Weekly goal setting
- Meals together
- Set days for field trips
- Areas designed for art/science/reading nooks, etc.

I generally avoided the blogs of the moms who seemed like they had everything together and their homes and homeschool rooms looked picture perfect. It's awesome if that's how you roll. I didn't.

Step 10: Avoid the Ten Biggest Blocks to Learning

Below are some of the biggest things that block the free flow of learning.

Fear: If you are feeling fearful, your kids will automatically pick up on it and become fearful themselves, So, when your inner GPS tells you that you are believing fearful thinking, pause and let your mind settle down.

Shame: Shame is the mistaken belief that "I am not good/worthy/lovable/smart." Because kids have been taught to compare themselves with others in school and to compete for the GPA, they often feel shame when they are not good at something or don't think that they compare favorably to their peers. Reassure them that the only person they are competing with is them self. Are they doing better today than yesterday? Is this something that they really care about and want to get good at?

Grades: Grades are silly. They don't accurately measure learning or capability. The top private schools in the country are currently engaged in an effort to replace grades with a Mastery Transcript. The state where we home educate requires letter grades for K-8 and then numeric grades and class ranking for grades 9-12. My daughters and I hold the grades lightly and know that they are not a measure of self-worth or innate capacity.

Comparison: Comparison is always a losing game. It will always get you tangled in a mess of negative thinking. Don't compare yourself to anyone else and don't compare your kids to anyone.

Time Pressure: Jo Boaler who teaches teachers how to teach math at Stanford says that timed math tests are the absolute worst way to learn maths. Timed tests of any sort are silly. Timetables for learning anything are also unscientific and invalid. So, let your children learn at their own pace guided by their inner wisdom. It really doesn't matter how old they are when they learn certain things. When something is relevant to their lives, they will dig in and learn it in a fraction of the time it would take if you forced them to learn it when they are neither interested nor ready.

Rote Memorization: It is helpful to have some things stored in our memory banks, like addresses, phone numbers, birthdays, recipes, etc. Memorization is a small sliver of the learning process. If you are using a curriculum that focuses mainly on filling your children with information that they need to regurgitate, I would invite you to find a learning resource that is actually about learning not memorizing.

Sitting Still: We are designed to move. Research has found that engaging the body during the learning process is not just helpful, it is required. Let your kids move when they want to move. It doesn't mean that they have ADHD, they are alive, energetic beings. Neurophysiologist and educator Carla Hannaford wrote a wonderful book on the subject called *Smart Moves*.

Focus on Mechanics Instead of Meaning: If you focus on "doing it right" instead of having fun doing it, you will kill the love of learning. Just like my daughter Kayli loves reading and writing, but learned to hate it in school, focusing on mechanics stifles the love of learning. Humans need to understand the relevance of something and make it meaningful to enjoy doing it. Parents continually asked Michael Jordan how to make their sons great basketball players. His response was always, "Let them learn to love basketball."

Mismatch of Learning Experience with Learning Style:

This is a big one! When my daughters were younger, we each did the Self-Portrait™ Power Traits Assessment. It was so helpful to figure out that they learned differently than I did. Somehow, it made my journey lighter and more fun. I realized I wasn't in charge. My oldest daughter learns through performing and doing. My youngest learns through reading and doing. I learn through reading and doing as well but with distinct differences.

I highly recommend doing the Self-Portrait™ Power Traits Assessment that my friend Mariaemma Willis and Victoria Hodson created. It was so helpful, I brought it into our homeschool resource center for all the parents. You can get $5 off with the links on my website for parents and students.

PART 5: The Emerging Educational Ecosystem

10 Principles for a Living Education Network

The organizations and resources I include in this section all align with the following principles.

1. The living education network is innovative, adaptive, and self-organizing.

2. The goal of education is free and empowered individuals who use their minds, creativity, and energy to co-create a free and fair society and healthy biosphere.

3. All levels of the education network are united around a shared cause of protecting every human's natural state of peace, joy, and wisdom while expanding wisdom, intelligence, critical thinking, kindness, and cooperation.

4. Relationships are at the center of thriving learning environments that catalyze collaboration. Teachers step into the roles of learning coaches and mentors. Families are the smallest learning unit. There are no threats.

5. Learning is emergent and soul-directed, not prescribed or predetermined. The focus of education is mastery of Self, the evolution of consciousness, and holistic wellbeing instead of information processing and mastery of subject matter.

6. Critical thinking and morality are developed through free inquiry into theosophy, philosophy, leading edge research and work in the new sciences, consciousness studies, and regenerative economics and business. Propaganda and all forms or indoctrination are removed from curriculum and teacher training.

7. Holistic systems are developed to demonstrate the capacity and know-how of learners -- replacing grades, GPA, standardized tests, and fixed degrees. Data mining of

learner activity, attitude, and social emotional factors is prohibited.

8. The definition of success expands to include the impact an individual has on the whole, including other people and the biosphere. Personal excellence replaces unbridled individual competition. Experiences and relationships are valued over the accumulation of stuff.

9. Command and control federal and state education bureaucracies that pursue efficiencies through economies of scale are transformed or replaced by more innovative, agile networks of interconnected local education webs which honor the richness and diversity of place.

10. Youth are encouraged to invest their time, energy, and money in their local communities instead of joining multi-national companies and overpriced, elite higher education institutions.

(There are many more options and they are growing all the time. I've only included my favorites.)

Local Homeschool Cooperatives

Most places have local homeschool cooperatives that meet once or twice a week. They are a great way to connect with other families. Many are religious and will require you to sign a statement that you adhere to their religious beliefs. Others are secular and inclusive. Search for "homeschool" in Facebook groups and you might be surprised how many homeschool groups are in your community.

Here are a few directories that you can check out:

The Homeschool Mom

Home EDucators Resource Directory

Homeschool Legal Defense Association

Self-Directed and Democratic Schools

The category of self-directed and democratic schools includes any learning environment where kids direct their own learning absent any adult coercion or agendas. You can find a list of schools self-directed.org and educationrevolution.org.

Agile Learning Centers

Agile Learning Centers are a network of self-directed learning centers that are growing in popularity. They address the no-form problem by using agile tools from software development. By carefully crafting the culture of the school and honoring individual choice, Agile Learning Centers don't use coercion to get kids to follow a pre-set agenda. If there isn't an ALC in your community, the ALC network has a ton of free resources to help you start one.

Prenda

Prenda is a network of microschools that started in Arizona and are now spreading through the country. You can start a Prenda microschool in your home or choose to homeschool your children at a neighborhood microschool. It's not unschooling, as they use online resources to cover reading, writing, math, grammar, etc. However, they do have a focus on projects and give kids a lot more freedom than schooling. It is free in Arizona and low cost elsewhere.

Sudbury Model

Sudbury Valley School Massachusetts is the original Sudbury school. A purely democratic model, decisions about running the school are made by voting and since students outnumber staff, the students essentially run the school.

Liberated Learners

Started by Ken Danforth, Liberated Learners is a network of alternative self-directed learning center for teens who don't want to do school. You can learn more at about their network at Liberated Learners.

Innovative Online Learning Opportunities

Outschool

Anyone with a passion or interest can teach a live video-based class for kids for ages 3-18 on Outschool. The teachers set the price and structure of each class. It could be a one-hour class on learning the multiplication tables or a semester long environmental science class. The classes are reviewed by the students, so there is a concerted effort to engage the kids and make it fun.

West River Academy

West River Academy turns life experience into academic credit. It is an accredited private school that offers enrollment, transcripts and high school graduation. You just need to check the homeschooling laws in your state to see if it meets the requirements. westriveracademy.com

Galileo

Galileo is an online self-directed school where kids do nanodegree programs each month based around a topic, and the kids join book, math and coding clubs that meet via video regularly. Like ALCs, they have daily check-in in the morning and then check-outs in the afternoon to see if they got done what they said they were going to do. Galileo has mentors that support the individual interests of the kids. Galileo recently merged with kids2market to offer an entrepreneurship program. Galileoxp.com

Sora Schools

Soraschools.com is an online project-based high school that was created by three friends who attended Georgia Tech and realized that high school was a bad experience for all of them. Their focus is helping kids to design passion-based projects and connecting kids with industry mentors. Teens learn as part of an engaged community. The founders did a year of intensive research to design high school from scratch without any assumptions of what it had to look like.

Alison
Alison offers free and low-cost online courses that will transfer to many colleges. Alison offers individual courses, learning paths, certificates, and degree programs. Alison.com

Secular Academic Homeschoolers
Secular Academic Homeschoolers offers a free and premium membership and online courses that are obviously focused on serious academics. The courses are structured like Outschool in that they have varying duration and prices.

School Beyond Limitations
School Beyond Limitations offers online learning experience for kids ages 10-18 who live in Europe. Classes are held from 9 am to 12 pm and are multidisciplinary. Each group of learners has two teachers: one that specializes in maths can science and the other in English and humanities. They also meet during the year in person three times for week-long experiences around Europe.

SchoolTeachers.com
SchoolTeachers.com offers online and self-paced classes with mentors who have subject area expertise. Your family can join for a monthly or annual membership that gives you access to all of the classes.

Khan Academy
I would be remiss if I didn't include Khan Academy because it offers a breadth of subjects, video instruction, progress tracking, and SAT/ACT prep. I tried Khan Academy with both of my daughters and they both hated it. And each learner is different.

Early College

One of the greatest benefits of learning outside of conventional schooling is that kids can start getting college credits so that they can lower their cost of college and graduate much earlier.

Most states offer free or reduced tuition to high school students who are doing dual enrollment at a community college. I recommend that if your child is doing dual enrollment, start with the common general education courses like ENG 101, ENG 201, Calculus, Foreign Languages, Introduction to Psychology, etc. You can see a list of General Education or Core Curriculum requirements at every college website. They vary widely across colleges and some GE requirements cannot be satisfied by dual enrollment courses.

My oldest daughter did a mix of college classes at the local community college and online college classes during her junior and senior years of high school. She will have completed two semesters of college credit before she applies to colleges.

Transfer of college credits is an interesting game. As long as you understand that the big freshman lecture courses are cash cows for colleges, you understand why they may not be overly excited about letting your kid opt out of them. That said, there are many colleges that are flexible and accommodating.

Jennifer Cook-DeRosa runs Homeschooling for College Credit and has Facebook groups that are specific to each state. This is a wonderful resource to get all of your questions answered.

Many students study for the College-Level Examination Programs (CLEP) or DSST, which are college-level tests that can be taken for college credit. Before you choose this path, it is helpful to know if your colleges of choice accept CLEP and/or DSST credits.

There are numerous companies that offer free and low-cost test prep services, including Study.com, Ron Paul Curriculum, and College Board.

Alternatives to College

One of the best alternatives is starting your own company or freelance business. It's interesting that college seems to be preparing people for jobs that no longer exist or are quickly disappearing, like college professors.

Great resources for Starting a Business
How to Build a Startup on Coursera is a free course from Lean Startup creator and Stanford professor, Steve Blank

Freelance University
Freelance University does just what its name implies. It offers courses to help people start and run a successful freelance business. It offers free workshops, a low-cost start-up program, and a membership plan that gives you access to all of their courses.

SV Academy
SV Academy offers a Tech Sales Certificate Program which can be done full-time over the course of 1 month or part-time for 3 months. It costs $10,000 for the program and access to the community. They will help place you in a job and have numerous industry partners. If you don't get a job, you will get a refund.

Praxis
Praxis offers a one-year business training and job placement program. They help young adults who choose not to go to college refine their personal brand, learning basic business and communication skills, and land a job in entry level jobs, primarily in sales or marketing. You only pay the Praxis fee once you get hired.

Crash
Crash spun out of Praxis and offers job seekers an alternative way to land a job that isn't the resume-job board path. They say it's the new way to find a job and their software platform helps job seekers develop pitches and demonstrate skills and capacities.

Brit + Co

If you love to craft and create, Brit + Co is a place to learn anything creative including flower arranging, cake decorating, digital marketing, and calligraphy. Passions can become micro businesses plus they fan the flames of creativity, so this is an interesting option that might turn into a viable source of income.

Lambda School

Lambda School offers courses in high-demand tech fields that are free until you land a job that pays more than $50,000. You sign an income share agreement when you enroll. Current classes are Data Science and Full Stack Web. The classes are online and live.

Unschooling Adventures

Travel is one of the best ways to educate yourself. Blake Boles offers big adventures to unschooling teenagers through Unschooling Adventures. Boles is a seasoned traveler and an indie guidance counselor to unschoolers.

Resources

There is an extensive list of resources on the Instead of Education page on CapriceThorsen.com with links.

Visit CapriceThorsen.com for links to resources, coaching, and online courses. Use code: creativity2020

Notes

[1] Maturana, Humberto. "Reflections by Humberto Maturana." *Systemic Design*, RSD5, Oct. 2016, systemic-design.net.

[2] Callaway, Ewen Nature Magazine. "Fearful Memories Passed Down to Mouse Descendants." *Scientific American*, 1 Dec. 2013, www.scientificamerican.com/article/fearful-memories-passed-down.

[3] Gordon, Mordechai. *Ten Common Myths in American Education*. Amsterdam-Netherlands, Netherlands, Amsterdam University Press, 2005, p. 37

[4] Ibid, p. 41

[5] *National Education Association*. National Education Association, nea.org. Accessed 26 June 2020,

[6] American Council of Trustees and Alumni. "A Crisis in Civic Education." *American Council of Trustees and Alumni*, Jan. 2016, www.goacta.org.

[7] Gallup. "Student Enthusiasm Falls as High School Graduation Nears." *Gallup*, 1 June 2017, gallup.com.

[8] Gallup. "Employee Engagement on the Rise in the U.S." *Gallup*, 26 Aug. 2018, gallup.com.

[9] Itzkowitz, Michael. "Higher Ed's Broken Bridge to the Middle Class – Third Way." *Third Way*, 25 Sept. 2019, www.thirdway.org/report/higher-eds-broken-bridge-to-the-middle-class.

[10] Dewey, John, and Philip Jackson. *The School and Society and The Child and the Curriculum (Centennial Publications of The University of Chicago Press)*. 1st ed., University of Chicago Press, 1991, p. 15

[11] American Humanist Association. "Definition of Humanism." *American Humanist Association*, 12 July 2020, americanhumanist.org/what-is-humanism/definition-of-humanism.

[12] American Humanist Association. "Humanist Manifesto I." *American Humanist Association*, 12 July 2020, americanhumanist.org/what-is-humanism/manifesto1.

[13] American Humanist. "AHA_v._BOP_Final_Settlement_All_Signatures." *American Humanist*, Mar. 2017, Americanhumanist.org.

[14] Organisation for Economic Co-operation and Development. "Programme for International Student Assessment (PISA) Results from PISA 2018." *Https://Www.Oecd.Org/*, 2019, www.oecd.org/pisa/publications/PISA2018_CN_USA.pdf

[15] "New Study of the Literacy of College Students Finds Some Are Graduating With Only Basic Skills." *American Institutes for Research*, 14 Sept. 2017, www.air.org/news/press-release/new-study-literacy-college-students-finds-some-are-graduating-only-basic-skills.

[16] Wylie Communications. "What's the Latest U.S. Literacy Rate?" *Wylie Communications*, Mar. 2019, www.wyliecomm.com/2019/03/us-literacy-rate.

[17] Gallup, "Student Enthusiasm Falls as High School Graduation Nears." *Gallup*, 1 June 2017, gallup.com.

[18] Wilson, Jackson, "Capturing students' attention: An empirical study", Journal of the Scholarship of Teaching and Learning, 12/01/2013

[19] American Institute for Research, New Study of the Literacy of College Students Finds Some Are Graduating With Only Basic Skills, 1/19/06, accessed on 11/18/19, https://www.air.org/news/press-release/new-study-literacy-college-students-finds-some-are-graduating-only-basic-skills

[20] Klein, A. (2015, April 10). No Child Left Behind: An Overview. *Education Week*. Retrieved 11/17/19 from https://www.edweek.org/ew/section/multimedia/no-child-left-behind-overview-definition-summary.html

[21] Sparks, S. (2019, October 30), 'No Progress' Seen in Reading or Math on Nation's Report Card, Education Week, retrieved 11/17/19 from http://blogs.edweek.org/edweek/inside-school-research/2019/10/reading_math_NAEP_2019.html

[22] Consortium for Policy Research in Education. "Seven Trends: The Transformation of the Teaching Force." *Cpre.Org*, Apr. 2014, www.cpre.org/sites/default/files/workingpapers/1506_7trendsapril2014.pdf.

[23] Becker, Jeff. "NASA 'Brainwaves Reveal Student Engagement, Operate Household Objects.'" *BrainCo*, 21 June 2019, www.brainco.tech/blog/2015/03/02/gaining-exposure.

[24] Ibid.

[25] Robinson, Melia. "Tech Billionaires Spent $170 Million on a New Kind of School — Now Classrooms Are Shrinking and Some Parents Say Their Kids Are 'Guinea Pigs.'" *Business Insider Nederland*, 22 Nov. 2017, www.businessinsider.nl/altschool-why-parents-leaving-2017-11?international=true&r=US.

[26] Strauss, Valerie. "Students Protest Zuckerberg-Backed Digital Learning Program and Ask Him: 'What Gives You This Right?'" *Washington Post*,

17 Nov. 2018, www.washingtonpost.com/gdpr-consent/?next_url=https%3a%2f%2fwww.washingtonpost.com%2feducatio n%2f2018%2f11%2f17%2fstudents-protest-zuckerberg-backed-digital-learning-program-ask-him-what-gives-you-this-right%2f, accessed 12/17/19

[27] Beckett, Lois. "Clear Backpacks, Monitored Emails: Life for US Students under Constant Surveillance." *The Guardian*, 10 Dec. 2019, www.theguardian.com/education/2019/dec/02/school-surveillance-us-schools-safety-shootings.

[28] Carnegie Mellon University - Heinz College. "Building Effective Communications Around Student Data Privacy—Executive Summary." *Https://Www.Studentprivacymatters.Org/*, 2017, www.studentprivacymatters.org/wp-content/uploads/2017/12/CMU-survey-privacy-start-ups-2017.pdf.

[29] Vozza, Stephanie. "It's Not Just You: These Super Successful People Suffer From Imposter Syndrome." *Fast Company*, 16 Aug. 2017, www.fastcompany.com/40447089/its-not-just-you-these-super-successful-people-suffer-from-imposter-syndrome.

[30] Dias, Brian G., and Kerry J. Ressler. "Parental Olfactory Experience Influences Behavior and Neural Structure in Subsequent GenerationsBrian G Dias1,2 & Kerry J, *Nature Neuroscience*, vol. 17, no. 1, 2014, www.nature.com/articles/nn.3594.epdf

[31] "The Odds Of You Being Alive Are Incredibly Small." *Business Insider*, 12 June 2012, www.businessinsider.com/infographic-the-odds-of-being-alive-2012-6?international=true&r=US&IR=T.

[32] "A Thousand Rivers." *Carol Black*, carolblack.org/a-thousand-rivers. Accessed 12 July 2020.

[33]"Roger J. Williams and the Science of Individuality." *Mises Institute*, 19 Aug. 2010, mises.org/library/roger-j-williams-and-science-individuality.

[34]hHogan Ph.D., Michael. "Collectivism and Individualism It's Not Either/or, It's Both." *Psychology Today*, 27 June 2019, www.psychologytoday.com/us/blog/in-one-lifespan/201906/collectivism-and-individualism.

[35] Gopnik, Alison. "Your Baby Is Smarter Than You Think." *Https://Www.Nytimes.Com/#publisher*, 17 Aug. 2009, www.nytimes.com/2009/08/16/opinion/16gopnik.html?pagewanted=1&_r=2&th&emc=th.

[36]Cook Moats, Louisa. "The Missing Foundation in Teacher Education: Knowledge of the Structure of Spoken and Written Language." *PA Coalition for World Class Math*, The Greenwood Institute, paworldclassmath.webs.com/Missing%20Foundation%20(Moats).pdf. Accessed 12 July 2020.

[37] Organisation for Economic Co-operation and Development. "Programme for International Student Assessment (PISA) Results from PISA 2018." *Https://Www.Oecd.Org/*, 2019, www.oecd.org/pisa/publications/PISA2018_CN_USA.pdf.

[38] Wylie Communications. "What's the Latest U.S. Literacy Rate?" *Wylie Communications*, Mar. 2019, www.wyliecomm.com/2019/03/us-literacy-rate.

[39] The Missing Foundation in Teacher Education: Knowledge of the Structure of Spoken and Written Language, Louisa Cook Moats, Annals of Dyslexia, 1994, https://paworldclassmath.webs.com/Missing%20Foundation%20(Moats).pdf, 12/29/19

[40] Tanya Chen, "Here's What Happens When A Bunch Of Adults Try To Do Fifth-Grade Math." *BuzzFeed*, 18 Dec. 2013, www.buzzfeed.com/tanyachen/heres-what-happens-when-a-bunch-of-adults-try-to-do-5th-grad.

[41] Gallup, Inc. "How Many Americans Know U.S. History? Part I." *Gallup.Com*, 14 Nov. 2018, news.gallup.com/poll/9526/How-Many-Americans-Know-US-History-Part.aspx.
In-text citation

[42] The National Education Association of the United States. "Cardinal Principles of Secondary Education: A Report, National Education Association of the United States. Commission on the Reorganization of Secondary Education: Free Download, Borrow, and Streaming :" *Internet Archive*, 1918, archive.org/details/cardinalprincipl00natiuoft/page/14/mode/2up

[43] American Council of Trustees and Alumni. "A Crisis in Civic Education." *American Council of Trustees and Alumni*, Jan. 2016, www.goacta.org.

[44] Skinner, Victor. "New Study Reveals Woeful State of American Civic Education." *EAGnews.Org*, 2 June 2020, www.eagnews.org/2016/01/new-study-reveals-woeful-state-of-american-civics-education.

Made in the USA
Las Vegas, NV
28 November 2022

60425070R00111